"If you feel lost in your own li[fe] pull over and wait for directions—not to drive faster or more frantically but to become comfortable with letting yourself feel lost for a while. Michelle is a good and safe person to sit with as you wait. I'm so grateful I did."

**Lisa-Jo Baker**, bestselling author of *Never Unfriended* and *Surprised by Motherhood*

"In *True You* Michelle DeRusha paints the ordinary world as something worthy of our attention, inviting us to uncover hidden beauty as we uncover within us the image of God. This journey to our truest self is paved with small moments, attentiveness, and gut-level honesty—payment we can all afford, though not without discomfort as we go. *True You* made me want to slow down, tell the truth, and set up camp in the wide, wild presence of God, where anything is possible. I am grateful for this luminous book."

**Shannan Martin**, author of *The Ministry of Ordinary Places* and *Falling Free*

"Michelle has done an incredible job of gently, practically, and beautifully teaching us to calm the restlessness within. So many of us sense there is not only more to life but more to us—we just haven't been taught how to create space for our true selves to thrive. This book is your guide to uncovering the pathway to who you were truly meant to be."

**Deidra Riggs**, author of *One* and *Every Little Thing*

"Ever since I began reading this book, I keep finding myself looking up at the trees. Not because this is a book about trees but because the trees hold compelling truths about what it means to live as my essential self. Michelle DeRusha uses words as if they are pruning shears—cutting away what gets in the way of *truest you* . . . what gets in the way of real intimacy with God. I was deeply moved by this book, which is rich with metaphor and incisive wisdom. At times I knew I needed to slow down my reading so that the truths might set in, yet I found myself utterly unable to resist turning the page. I didn't want this book to end and will return to its pages again and again. I highly recommend *True You*."

Jennifer Dukes Lee, author of *It's All Under Control* and *The Happiness Dare*

"Captivating and convicting, *True You* is a beautiful discovery on how to come home to one's true self. Writing with a caretaker's heart, Michelle DeRusha is a compassionate, hopeful voice coaxing us to stop, beckoning us to see, reminding us of the truth, and leading us toward rest. In a noisy world consumed with busyness, this book will help you think about silence and solitude differently."

Shelly Miller, author of *Rhythms of Rest: Finding the Spirit of Sabbath in a Busy World*

"This book stopped me in my tracks. I'm a huge fan of Henri Nouwen, and the same gentle spirit he wrote with can be found in the pages of DeRusha's *True You*. She challenges our culture of busyness with such kindness and grace, inviting us instead of guilting us, showing us that all is well on the quiet, simple path. I can't recommend this book enough."

Shawn Smucker, author of *Once We Were Strangers*

"Pruning is a powerful metaphor for spiritual transformation, but our understanding of it is too often superficial. Michelle DeRusha gives depth and richness to a familiar theme, and the result is a book of rare wisdom and insight. *True You* is a book about the necessity of silence, solitude, and stillness, but it is written by someone with little natural affinity for those contemplative spiritual practices. The result is a compelling personal story shared with rare candor that reveals an accessible path toward deeper intimacy with God. This is a book for hungry, restless souls."

Christie Purifoy, author of *Roots and Sky* and *Placemaker*

# true you

LETTING GO OF YOUR FALSE SELF TO
UNCOVER THE PERSON GOD CREATED

## Michelle DeRusha

**BakerBooks**

*a division of Baker Publishing Group*
Grand Rapids, Michigan

Published by Baker Books
a division of Baker Publishing Group
PO Box 6287, Grand Rapids, MI 49516-6287
www.bakerbooks.com

Printed in the United States of America

Library of Congress Cataloging-in-Publication Data
Names: DeRusha, Michelle, author.
Title: True you : letting go of your false self to uncover the person God created / Michelle DeRusha.
Description: Grand Rapids, MI : Baker Books, [2019]
Identifiers: LCCN 2018020588 | ISBN 9780801077913 (pbk. : alk. paper)
Subjects: LCSH: Spirituality—Christianity. | Spiritual life—Christianity. | Self-actualization (Psychology)—Religious aspects—Christianity.
Classification: LCC BV4501.3 .D476 2019 | DDC 248.4—dc23
LC record available at https://lccn.loc.gov/2018020588

Some names and details have been changed to protect the privacy of the individuals involved.

The author is represented by the literary agency of Books & Such Literary Management.

19  20  21  22  23  24  25      7  6  5  4  3  2  1

For Noah and Rowan

Slowly
she celebrated the sacrament of *letting go*
first she surrendered her *green*
then the *orange, yellow,* and *red*
finally she let go of her *brown*
shedding her last leaf
she stood empty and silent, stripped bare.[1]

—From Macrina Wiederkehr,
*Seasons of Your Heart*

I've been out of step with you for a long time,
in the wrong since before I was born.
What you're after is truth from the inside out.
Enter me, then; conceive a new, true life.

—Psalm 51:6 Message

# contents

Acknowledgments   9

Introduction: *A Tale of Two Trees*   13

**Part 1:  Know the Tree**

   1.  Leaves and Branches: *How We Clutter Our Lives,*
       *Minds, and Souls*   23

   2.  Beneath the Canopy: *Hearing What's Been There*
       *All Along*   41

   3.  Broken Limbs: *Do You Want to Get Well?*   57

   4.  Seeds of Desire: *Facing Your Deepest*
       *Brokenness*   77

**Part 2:  *Fukinaoshi* of the Soul**

   5.  The Hard Prune: *Letting Go of the Last*
       *Handhold*   97

   6.  The Far Side of the Wilderness: *Following God,*
       *Even When You Can't See the Way Through*   117

7. Rooted: *Practicing the Discipline of Staying in Place*   135

**Part 3:  Shaping**

8. Twine and Splint: *Two Steps Forward, One Step Back*   157
9. Way Opens: *On Coming Alive*   177
10. Water, Wood, Air, and Stone: *We Are Better Together*   197

Epilogue   219
Appendix   223
Notes   227

# acknowledgments

This book was a long time in the making, which means I am grateful to a whole lot of people who helped all along the way.

Chad Allen—I wouldn't be anywhere close to this point in my journey as an author if it wasn't for you. Thank you for always being in my corner.

To Michelle Rapkin—I knew we were a good fit from our first telephone conversation (and the fact that you are two "*l*'s" too). Thank you for your insightful editing and for all you did to help make this book shine.

To the Baker Books editorial and marketing teams—Rebecca Guzman, Jessica English, Julie Davis, Mark Rice, Erin Smith, Abby Van Wormer, Brianne Dekker, and Patti Brinks. Thank you for your pursuit of excellence. Your creativity, talent, and input made all the difference.

To my agent, Rachelle Gardner—you gently prodded me to work and rework the proposal for this book again and again.

Thank you for your perseverance, for your refusal to submit something that's "good enough," for your astute insights, and for your uncanny ability to know what's working and what's not. I am so grateful for you!

To my Tuscany Writers Retreat fellow sojourners, especially Jenni Burke and Jamin Goggin—thank you for receiving my brokenness with compassion and love. Thank you for being a window into God's presence when I couldn't see.

To my blog and *Back Patio* newsletter readers and subscribers— we've been together for the long haul, and I couldn't be more grateful for your support and encouragement. Thank you especially for your uplifting comments and emails when I hit the writing wall with this book. Your encouragement helped me keep my fingers on the keyboard.

To the #LNK Blog Love Writers—first of all, where in the world did we get that wonky name? Seriously, though, you ladies are the best! I so look forward to our monthly meet-ups— it's so good to gather with a group of like-minded writers who "get it." Thanks, too, for teaching this Latest Adopter Ever how to Insta-story!

To Lynn Morrissey—thank you for sharing a bit of your story with me and for helping me grapple my way through the "Twine and Splint" chapter. Mostly, though, thank you for being *you*—one of the most encouraging, supportive people I've ever had the delight to know.

To Deidra Riggs—thank you for being my person in more ways than I can count.

*acknowledgments*

To my parents, Maureen and Brad DeRusha—for always reminding me that I am loved.

To Brad, Noah, and Rowan—I know I always say Josie is my favorite, but we all know that's not true. You are my favorites by a million miles, and I love you more than words can convey.

# introduction

## A tale of two trees

Oak trees are always the last to lose their leaves. I never noticed this phenomenon until I began a daily practice of sitting still. It all began with a whim. One sunny November afternoon while I was walking my dog, I decided to stop and sit on a park bench. The bench, a simple, dark green metal lattice seat, was new. It had appeared at the edge of the walking path earlier that summer, fastened onto a freshly poured slab of concrete, a bronze memorial plaque fixed beneath it. The spot overlooked a small ravine, a couple of oak trees, a Scotch pine, and a trickling creek. In the summer the grassy hillside is speckled with black-eyed Susans, purple coneflower, and Queen Anne's lace, but by the time I first sat on the park bench in late autumn, the wildflowers had died off. All that remained were patches of crisp tallgrass, windblown stalks, and a dry streambed.

13

As I rested there for a few minutes with Josie sprawled at my feet, I decided I would make this bench-sitting part of my daily routine. I vowed I would stop at that same spot along our walking route every day, and I would sit for five minutes. I would sit in silence, I determined—without music or a podcast in my ears; without dialing my mother or texting my sister; without snapping photos with my camera phone or scrolling through Instagram or Facebook. I would simply sit in silence for five minutes. I figured it would be good for me to take a tiny breather in each hectic day.

The first afternoon I sat on the park bench, I looked at my watch after two minutes and then again after four. When I shifted my weight, I felt the chill of the metal seat through my jeans. I crossed and uncrossed my legs, bent down to pet the dog, and stared at the ravine as the cool breeze blew strands of hair across my face. Turns out, five minutes on a park bench sounds short in principle but is a surprisingly long time in reality.

The next day during my five minutes at the bench, I took a cue from Josie, who sat still, ears pricked, nose quivering. I looked at what she looked at; I sniffed, trying to smell what she smelled. When she twitched her ears, I turned my head too, attempting to hear what she'd heard. I noticed a little more of my surroundings that second day, like the fact that the leaves of the burr oak on the edge of the ravine still clung stubborn and tenacious to the branches. Unlike the maples, birches, elms, and ash trees, which had dropped their leaves like colorful confetti more than a month ago, the oaks were still fully dressed, their dry leaves scraping together in the wind like sandpaper.

I also noticed something about myself on that second day. Sitting on a bench right there in the open alongside the path, I realized I felt unexpectedly and oddly vulnerable. It felt a little foolish to be doing nothing but staring into space, feeling the slippery softness of the pine needles under my feet, listening to the leaves. I was grateful that section of the path is not well traveled. I didn't want to see someone I knew, or even for a stranger to notice me and think I was some kind of crazy lady, sniffing at the air and shuffling my shoes. It was already obvious to me on that second day of sitting that the quiet and stillness made me uncomfortable, although I couldn't put my finger on exactly why.

I wasn't at all sure what I was doing there, just sitting. All I knew was that I felt compelled to do it, even though I didn't particularly like it, and even though I knew, after only two days, that I would resist it in the coming weeks. At the same time, I knew this sitting in stillness was something I had to do. Somehow I knew that the stopping—the interruption to my daily routine and my incessant push to get from Point A to Point B—was important, maybe even imperative.

Turns out, I learned over the weeks and months of sitting in quiet solitude that I am a lot like the oak tree that clings so fiercely to its leaves. I suspect a lot of us are. We, too, clutch our camouflage—the person we present to the world, to our own selves, and even to God. We, too, are unwilling to shed our false selves, to let go, to live vulnerably and authentically. We are afraid of what might happen if we drop our protective cover, afraid of how we could be seen or perceived, or how we may see or perceive our own selves. We are leery of what we may discover under all those layers. We spend a great deal of our time and energy holding tight-fisted to our leaves, simply because we are too afraid to let go, too afraid of what, or who, we will find underneath.

Sitting in silence every day helped me see that my "leaves" of choice are busyness and productivity, drive and efficiency, achievement and success. I used those "leaves" to insulate me from my own deepest self, because, although I didn't realize it consciously, I was afraid of what was underneath. I was afraid of who I would find if I began to prune away my layers of self-protection. And so I clung with an iron grip to my false self, to the false identity I'd meticulously crafted over the years. I was busy, productive, and driven. I pushed myself to accomplish, achieve, and succeed. *That's just who I am*, I often told myself. *That's just how I was made.*

I suspect I'm not alone in my tendency to hide. Perhaps you, too, are clinging to your own array of brittle branches and desiccated leaves—using your false identity or even your daily routines and bad habits to hide from something. Perfectionism, workaholism, procrastination, consumerism, materialism—even substance abuse and addiction—are all different kinds of "leaves," different methods of self-protection, different ways we have of hiding and avoiding.

Perhaps you, like me, are evading something. Perhaps you are estranged from your truest, deepest self. And perhaps you, like me, haven't the foggiest idea how to prune away your deadwood and begin to dismantle the structure you've built over a lifetime. My hope is that this book will help you begin that process. My hope is that you will join me on the journey toward uncovering the uniquely beautiful person God created you to be.

Two years ago on a warm June morning, my husband, our two boys, and I met Marsha, a volunteer guide, just inside the front gate of the Portland Japanese Garden. We were at the end of a ten-day vacation to the Pacific Northwest, and I was eager to introduce my family to this special place that I had discovered years before on a work trip. As we followed Marsha across petite wooden bridges, along winding paths, and over stepping-stones set into spongy moss, I remembered how the garden seemed to wrap its visitors in a shawl of quiet. We spoke in whispers as we strolled, a lullaby of flowing water melding with the rhythmic crunch of gravel beneath our shoes.

Marsha paused beside a large Japanese maple poised regal and elegant like a grand dame on a small, moss-covered hill, and as we waited for the rest of our group to catch up, I gazed at the tree. Its delicate chartreuse leaves fanned like antique lace over an elaborate network of dark limbs and branches that spread like veins beneath the canopy. When the stragglers joined us, Marsha explained that a particular Japanese gardening technique called "open center pruning" was responsible not only for the sculptural appeal of this maple, but also for the uncluttered space and serenity in the garden as a whole.

When a Japanese gardener "prunes open," Marsha explained, he or she cuts away not only dead branches and foliage, but also often a number of perfectly healthy branches that detract from the beauty inherent in the tree's essential structure. Pruning open allows the visitor to see up, out, and beyond the trees to the sky, creating a sense of spaciousness and letting light into the garden. It also enables an individual tree to flourish by removing complicating elements, simplifying structure, and revealing its essence. The process of pruning open turns the tree inside out, so to speak, revealing the beautiful design inherent within it. Sometimes, Marsha said, the process of pruning open requires a major restructuring—cutting back limbs and dramatically altering the form of the tree—while other times, only a gentler, more subtle reshaping is necessary.

Our group continued on with the tour, but I held back, reluctant to leave this one captivating tree. I circled it, snapping photographs, trying somehow to capture its enchanting beauty and gracefulness. There was something mesmerizing about the tree, the way its limbs and branches spread like an elaborate scaffolding beneath its intricate canopy of delicate green, the way its roots, gnarled and exposed, gripped the mossy hill. I yearned to lean my body against its twisting trunk, to soak up the wisdom I sensed coursing deep within it.

Eventually I ran to catch up with my family, but even after the tour had ended, I found myself still thinking about that one tree. In the months that followed our visit, I thought a lot about the practice of pruning open, and I've since come to understand it as a beautiful metaphor—one we can look to for guidance in our own lives and along our own spiritual journeys.

The practice of pruning open is not an easy one. In both gardening and in life, it's a skill that takes discipline, insight, and years of trial and error, and in many ways, it goes against the grain. Metaphorically speaking, pruning is the antithesis of contemporary western culture. It is the path toward smaller, rather than larger; toward quiet, rather than loud; toward slow, rather than fast; toward simple, rather than busy; toward dismantling, rather than building; toward less, rather than more. Pruning may not be a popular practice—at least according to what our bigger-better-faster-more society values—but it is an essential one, not only for trees, but also for ourselves and particularly for our souls. It is only in moving toward smaller and less—in cutting back in order to open up—that we uncover who we are at the very center of our God-created selves.

The truth is, God does not wish for us to stand stubborn like the autumn oak tree, cloaked in a façade of protection, our truest, most authentic selves obscured beneath a tangled bramble of false security. Rather, he desires us to live like the Japanese maple tree, our true essence revealed and flourishing, our true self front and center, secure and thriving. God yearns for us to live wholeheartedly and truthfully as the unique, beautiful, beloved individuals he created us to be. Most of all, God's deepest desire is for us to know him, to root our whole selves in him like a tree rooted by a stream, and to know his deep, abiding love for us. God yearns for us to live in the spacious, light-filled freedom of Christ and to know ourselves in him, through him, and with him.

> It is only in moving toward smaller and less—in cutting back in order to open up—that we uncover who we are at the very center of our God-created selves.

As you let go of your false self, branch by branch, leaf by leaf, and layer by layer—as you finally begin to relinquish, open up, and allow God to prune you from the inside out—you will grow in ways you never imagined: in your relationships with loved ones; in connection with and love for your neighbors; in your vocation; in your heart, mind, and soul; and in intimacy with God himself. Your true, essential self, the *you* uniquely created by God, is there, deep inside you, hidden beneath layer upon layer of leaves clinging fast. Like the elegant Japanese maple tree, a spacious place is waiting to be revealed, and exuberant life is waiting to unfurl and blossom.

Pruning open is the way in.

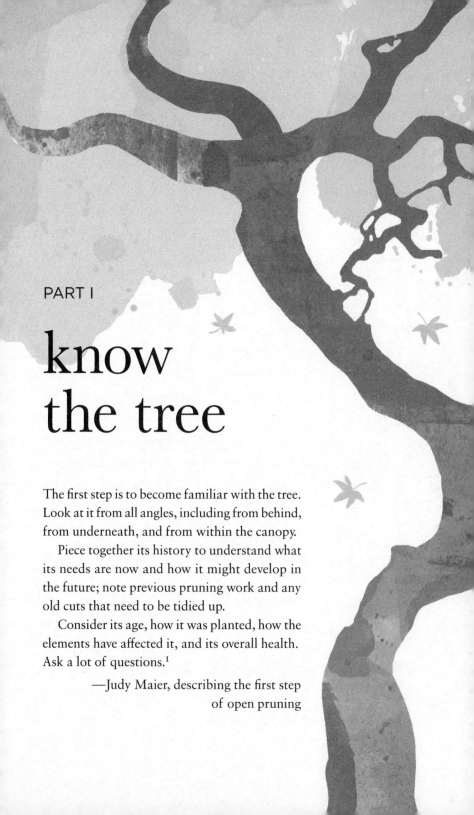

PART I

# know
# the tree

The first step is to become familiar with the tree.
Look at it from all angles, including from behind,
from underneath, and from within the canopy.

Piece together its history to understand what
its needs are now and how it might develop in
the future; note previous pruning work and any
old cuts that need to be tidied up.

Consider its age, how it was planted, how the
elements have affected it, and its overall health.
Ask a lot of questions.[1]

—Judy Maier, describing the first step
of open pruning

# 1

# leaves and branches

## How we clutter our lives, minds, and souls

> We are merely moving shadows,
> and all our busy rushing ends in nothing.
> —Psalm 39:6 NLT

On January 12, 2007, a young man dressed in a gray, long-sleeve T-shirt, jeans, and a baseball cap emerged from the metro at the L'Enfant Plaza station in Washington, tucked a violin under his chin, and began to play. The violinist performed six classical pieces in 43 minutes, during which time 1,097 commuters passed him. Seven of those people stopped what they were doing to stand and listen for at least one minute; one young boy craned his neck to catch a glimpse of the musician as his mother led him by the hand out of the station; and 27 people threw money into the open violin case at the musician's feet as they passed. That means 1,070 people hurried by without as much as a glance at the violinist. Those talking on cell phones or with earbuds in their ears didn't even hear him.

Turns out, most of the people who dashed through the metro station that morning on the way to work had no idea that the musician playing next to the trash can was none other than renowned virtuoso Joshua Bell, performing on his 1713, $3.5 million Stradivarius violin.

Bell's performance was arranged by the *Washington Post Magazine* as "an experiment in context, perception and priorities." Editors at the magazine were interested in one question in particular: "In a banal setting at an inconvenient time, would beauty transcend?"[1]

Prior to the incognito performance, Leonard Slatkin, director of the National Symphony Orchestra, had predicted that Bell's impeccable playing would attract people passing through the station, even if they didn't recognize the musician himself. "My guess is there might be 35 or 40 who will recognize the quality for what it is. Maybe 75 to 100 will stop and spend some time listening," he told journalist Gene Weingarten.[2] In preparing for the event, *Washington Post Magazine* editors were concerned about crowd control. They figured at least several people would recognize Bell, stop to listen, and then attract other listeners.

Turns out there was no need for concern.

When he watched the video of the experiment later, Bell said he wasn't surprised he didn't draw a crowd in the middle of rush hour. He was, however, surprised by the number of people who didn't appear to notice him at all. It was as if he was invisible, Bell observed. He wondered if maybe the commuters ignored him so they wouldn't have to feel guilty about not throwing money into his open violin case. But when reporters questioned passersby later, no one gave that reason for not stopping to listen. "People just said they were busy, had other things on their mind. Some who were on cellphones spoke louder as they passed Bell, to compete with that infernal racket."[3]

The article about the experiment notes that there was no ethnic or demographic pattern to differentiate between the few who stayed to watch Bell from the vast majority who hurried by. The behavior of only one demographic was consistent through the 43 minutes: "Every single time a child walked past, he or she tried to stop and watch. And every single time, a parent scooted the kid away."[4]

I watched clips from Bell's Metro station performance on my laptop. Even on the choppy recording, the sound of his violin is lush and rich, and Bell's playing is mesmerizing as he moves along with the music, like a reed swaying in a breeze. I don't know much about classical music, but I know enough to recognize a stellar performance when I hear it.

I'd like to think I would have been one of the seven people who stopped to listen to one of the greatest classical musicians in the world play a free concert in a Washington, DC, train station. I'd like to think I would have been the mom who paused with her child for at least a minute or two to listen, entranced, before scurrying toward the exit. But I know myself better than that. I'm pretty sure I, too, would have hurried past Joshua Bell playing Franz Schubert's "Ave Maria" on his 1713 Stradivarius violin. I might have cast him a curious glance, but I would have kept right on going, bent on arriving at my destination, tackling my to-do list, and accomplishing whatever pressing tasks awaited me that day.

## Hustling for Self-Worth

"Hustle!!!"

I hear my father's voice over the clash of shin pads and the scuffle of cleats, over the instructions shouted from my coach on the sideline and the grunts of my fellow players as they tussle for the ball, bodies banging up against one another. The command comes at regular intervals, regardless of whether I'm lagging or not. "Hustle, Shelly, hustle!!" And I do. I hustle, springing after the soccer ball, challenging defensive opponents twice my size, refusing to flinch when the ball is kicked square at my face.

Later, after the game has ended, I drift a few steps behind my parents as we walk toward the parking lot, eavesdropping on the dads. "What do you feed her before the game, raw meat?" the father of one of my teammates jokes. My dad laughs, proud.

I toss my ball into the trunk of the car, slide into the backseat, and roll down the window. As I lean back, I catch my dad's eyes in the rearview mirror. "Good hustle out there, Shelly; way to make it happen." I beam back at him. My dad is pleased with my performance. I am tired but happy.

Truth be told, I hustled on and off the soccer field throughout my childhood and young adulthood—and not just to please my father. I don't know if it's a product of nature or nurture or a combination of both, but I've been driven to produce, achieve, and succeed for as long as I can remember.

"Make it happen" was a directive repeated often in my house when I was growing up, and it's a mantra I've chanted in my head ever since.

I got my first job in the fourth grade, when the neighbor boy who lived two houses down sold me his newspaper route. Six afternoons a week, rain, wind, snow, or sunshine, I pulled a stack of the *Springfield Union-News* in a red Radio Flyer wagon (a sled if the snow was deep) up one side of our street and down the other, sliding the afternoon edition under front mats, into mailboxes, and behind screen doors. I lived for Christmas, the season of big tips: five dollars slipped into an envelope, occasionally a crisp ten. After a few years I outgrew the red wagon, and, taller and stronger, carried the papers house to house and street to street in a grungy bag worn across my body from shoulder to thigh, the canvas, like my palms, smeared gray with newsprint.

I got my first real job when I was a sophomore in high school. A couple of days a week after school I walked down Maple Street to the local nursing home, where I changed into my "uniform"—white cotton skirt, white shoes, white T-shirt, and hairnet. I worked the dinner shift in the kitchen, Saran-wrapping plated egg salad sandwiches, sliding plastic racks of dirty dishes and trays into the steaming dishwasher, and unloading scalding silverware.

I was one of those teenagers who was involved in everything—sports, clubs, social events, work—and still earned good grades, not so much because I was academically gifted, but simply because I hustled, studying hours every night after getting home from work or soccer or track practice. I "made it happen." My parents had high expectations of me as a student, but my motivation ran deeper than their approval. I was driven to achieve because success made me feel valuable and important. I liked the awards I racked up. I enjoyed seeing my name listed as an honor roll student in the local newspaper every semester. I kept myself busy, motivated, and focused because the results of my efforts—success and achievement—filled, at least temporarily, a seemingly insatiable desire not only to be known, but to be recognized and admired.

I graduated from high school more than three decades ago, and although a lot about me has changed since then, in many ways, I am still very much the same person, driven to achieve and succeed. I'm type A through and through—or, to be more exact, triple type A, as my husband, Brad, jokes. I'm a Three on the Enneagram personality typing system— "Achiever/Performer: success-oriented, pragmatic, adaptable, excelling, driven, and image-conscious."[5] According to the Gallup StrengthsFinder Assessment, my top five strengths are Achiever, Activator, Focus, Discipline, and Responsibility. You get the picture.

I worked at several different jobs after finishing my college degree—magazine editor, communications director, public relations specialist—but I found my sweet spot when I landed a communications job at a Fortune 500 financial services company. Most of my colleagues were new parents at the time, and as they hurried out the door at 5:30 p.m. to retrieve their kids from after-school care and prepared to shuttle them back and forth to their evening activities, I stayed at my desk. I didn't yet have children, and I was eager to please my boss by putting in extra hours and working later than everyone else in my department. I was determined to get ahead of my peers, and, truth be told, I thrived in the competitive environment, where raises were based on merit and climbing the corporate ladder was not only expected but encouraged.

"They're not going anywhere in this place," my boss muttered one evening, shaking her head as the last of her staff grabbed their coats and lunch bags and darted out the door. "You, on the other hand," she said, turning toward me as I sat hunched in my cubicle. "I've got my eye on you for the fast track." I remember how pleased I felt, how I smiled inside when she said that—"the fast track." I vowed to make it happen—to work harder, stay later, and take on more. The corporate ladder rose glittering before me, and I couldn't climb it fast enough.

I didn't end up staying in that job as long as I would have liked. Barely six months after I started, my husband, who had recently completed his doctorate, landed a position as an English professor at a small liberal arts college in Nebraska. We moved from Massachusetts to Lincoln in 2001, and shortly after, we had our first child.

With a new baby (and another to follow three years later), it looked like my days of scaling the corporate ladder were over. Instead, I took a part-time job as a fund-raising writer at a nonprofit, and then, several years after moving to Nebraska, I also did something I'd never done before: I started writing in my free time. Over the course of two and a half years I wrote my first book during the fringe hours, mainly on my days off while the kids were napping and during the early mornings when the house was quiet. My professional ambitions had changed, but, as I quickly discovered, the publishing industry had a ladder too, and I set my sights on the top rung. My goal was to become a successful, published author, and I was determined to make it happen.

Years after hustling on the soccer field, in the classroom, and in the workplace, my specific priorities had changed, but my overall end goal was still the same: to succeed and achieve. And while it was no longer the grade on the top of a quiz, the score emblazoned on a board, or the next job promotion that motivated me, my definition of success was still largely based on numbers. As a writer with a goal of publication, I turned my attention to growing my number of blog subscribers and website page views, as well as the number of social media followers, shares, and retweets my posts earned. Once my first book released, I relentlessly tracked its rank on Amazon. I was still focused on "making it happen"—the "it" being success as a published author— and I was more driven, more obsessed, than ever.

I cringe now to admit this, but there were seasons in my publishing journey in which I monitored the Amazon rank not only of my own book, but of my peers' books too, as well as stats like the number of times their blog posts were shared on social media—even writers I respect, admire, and with whom I am friends. Subsequently I vacillated daily, sometimes hourly, between euphoria when my numbers measured up and despair when they didn't. I looked to the numbers to determine my value and worth.

Hustle, productivity, busyness, and striving to achieve make up a lot of leaves and branches on my tree. I've dedicated significant mental and physical energy to these pursuits over the years, and they've taken up a lot of space in my soul. I've hustled so long for my self-worth, it's become a habit deeply ingrained in me. I had no idea how destructive this habit was to my sense of self and to my relationship with God. I walked to the drumbeat of busyness for so long, I didn't realize it was detrimental both to my self-identity and to the well-being of my soul.

Turns out, I'm not alone. Our culture values busyness, achievement, efficiency, and productivity above all else. We are taught from our youngest days to produce, and we are rewarded for our efforts and accomplishments. Many of us wear our busyness as a badge of honor, proud at the end of the day of the number of items we've ticked off our to-do list. Ask virtually any woman and most men these days, "How are you?" and their answer is likely to be "Busy" or "Crazy busy." For a while, always aiming to one-up my peers, my answer to that question was "Insanely busy."

## The Badge of Busyness

Americans in particular base their self-value on their level of productivity and their accomplishments. Consider, for instance, the most recent research on how we spend our leisure time . . . or rather, how we don't. Fifty-four percent of Americans left vacation time unused in 2016, adding up to a record-setting 662 million unused vacation days. Even when we do take vacation, we are worried about the impact of time off on our job security. Twenty-six percent of Americans polled in a 2016 survey said they feared taking vacation could make them appear less dedicated at work, while 21 percent expressed concern that taking time off would impact their eligibility for a raise or promotion. There is, however, some slightly better news than in previous years. In 2016, average vacation use increased to 16.8 days per worker, compared to 16.2 days in 2015, marking the first uptick since vacation usage began its rapid decline in 2000. (To offer some perspective, between 1976 and 2000, the long-term average vacation usage was 20.3 days per year.)[6]

Clearly many of us are defined by our busyness, and we are only getting busier. At the same time, that hustle is of a particular nature. The kind of busy I'm talking about here—and believe me, I'm as guilty as anyone—is largely voluntary and self-imposed. We mindlessly check our email thirty times a day; we scroll half a dozen social media apps while we wait in the doctor's office or the grocery store check-out line; we take on yet another work project that will mean extra hours in the office; we say yes to another committee, event, or volunteer opportunity; we drive our kids to one more extracurricular activity; we surf the internet until all hours of the night looking for the latest fill-in-the-blank item we absolutely must have.

Part of our need to be busy and productive (or at the very least look that way) comes from our desire to be valued and known. If we are busy, we must be needed, and if we are needed, we must be important. We also like the hit of adrenaline that courses through our veins when we are maxed-out in super-productivity mode. At the end of the day, seeing a perfect black line crossing out each item on my to-do list gives me a high like virtually nothing else. And this high isn't imagined; it's the result of a real chemical reaction. Busyness can be addictive, triggering the release of dopamine, the brain chemical that's responsible for the feeling of well-being we experience after an especially productive work session.

As mindfulness expert Gillian Coutts explains, "We can be as addicted to action as much as any other type of stimulant or habit."[7] Accomplishing even small, superfluous tasks delivers a rush of dopamine, which, in turn, prompts the brain to desire another hit and then another in order to maintain a sense of gratification. Before long, we find ourselves caught in the cycle of addiction, except instead of needing alcohol, or nicotine, or a new pair of Uggs, we need to be constantly busy—moving, doing, and producing.

This addiction to busyness is devastating to our souls. "Our world will divert your soul's attention because it is a cluttered world," says author John Ortberg. "And clutter is maybe the most dangerous result, because it's so subtle."[8] He's right; clutter is subtle because it's easy to justify: just one more item, one more activity, one more errand, one more email. "More" comes one small thing or one obligation at a time, until before you know it, it's become more, more, more. Clutter is subtle until suddenly it's a mountain you can't dig out from under.

Part of our need to be busy and productive comes from our desire to be valued and known. If we are busy, we must be needed, and if we are needed, we must be important.

Ortberg uses the parable of the scattered seed in the Gospel of Mark to illustrate his point. The cluttered soul, he says, is like the seed that falls among the thorns and is eventually choked out by the weeds. "The busy soul gets attached to the wrong things, because the soul is sticky," Ortberg explains. "The Velcro of the soul is what Jesus calls 'desire.'"[9]

We may desire money, like the rich man who asks Jesus, "What must I do to inherit eternal life?" (Mark 10:17; see 10:17–31 for context). Or we may desire less tangible things, like power, success, recognition, or fame. Not only does the clutter of the world—the stuff we think we need to buy and the things we think we need to do—tempt us to covet, it also distracts us from the deeper soul work we should be pursuing. Like the crow that's attracted to the glittery ribbon, we are wooed by shallow glitz and thus neglect the deeper contemplation necessary for spiritual growth.

## The Busy Brain

Recently my son Noah and I walked out to Artist's Point, a rocky outcropping on the shore of Lake Superior in northern Minnesota. Though it was summertime, a cold breeze blew off the frigid water, so we searched for a spot to sit that would be protected from the wind. After a bit of scrambling over the rocks, we found a sheltered nook between two large boulders. Nestled into our cozy hollow, the sun warm on my face, I pulled a book from my bag and opened it on my lap. "You should have brought something to read," I said, turning to Noah. He shook his head no. "I don't always have to have a book," he said. "Mostly I'm happy just to sit."

The thing is, I always have to have a book. Or a notebook. Or my phone. Or my to-do list. I need *something* to do, even if only to fill five minutes. I hesitate to admit this, but I frequently pull out my phone to check my email while waiting at a red light. How long does it take for a light to change? A minute? Two? And yet, I can't sit unbusy for even that brief period. Part of the impulse to reach for my phone is habit, yet at the same time, I feel a pressing almost desperate need to be productive, to "make good use of my time." I simply can't bear not being busy, or at the very least, occupied.

Neuroscientist Caroline Leaf explains why. The brain, Dr. Leaf notes, is composed of networks that function together. The network responsible for the nonconscious part of the brain (called the *default mode network*, or DMN) operates 24 hours a day and is where thinking, building, and sorting thoughts takes place. The DMN is also where the brain engages in what Leaf calls "intrinsic activity" or "directed rest"—activities like contemplation, daydreaming, introspection, and sleeping. When we switch off from busyness mode, which takes place in what's called the *task positive network* (TPN)—the conscious part of our brain that supports the active thinking required to make decisions—and transition into the more contemplative state of directed rest in DMN, we appear to slow down physically, but our mental resources actually speed up and our thinking moves to a higher level. [10]

Dr. Leaf describes the activation of the DMN as a "Sabbath in the brain." In this state of directed rest, you outwardly appear to slow down, but inwardly, your mental resources increase as your brain engages in the deep work of ruminating, imagining, and self-reflecting. Dr. Leaf points out that brain imaging of people who regularly practice meditation—that is, people who regularly engage in directed rest—indicates a more active DMN, with the brain "growing more branches and integrating and linking thoughts, which translates as increased intelligence and that wonderful feeling of peace."[11]

When we don't slow down and enter this rest state, we disrupt the natural functioning of the brain. The beautifully harmonized system goes awry, when, instead of entering into directed rest on a regular basis, we constantly and relentlessly activate the TPN, which results in action—busyness—as well

as, if left unchecked, an inward feeling of anxiety, restlessness, and discontent. In other words, our mind needs time
and space to catch up with what our soul already knows.

Decision making and action are obviously necessary for
our survival and livelihood, but not *all the time*. If we fail
to activate the DMN on a regular basis and
instead constantly push the TPN part of our
brain to keep working, busyness can become
our default mode. That's why we can sometimes feel like we're on autopilot when we
are busy, and also why we can feel uncomfortable or even anxious or agitated when
we're supposed to be resting or relaxing. If
we've trained it to be busy at all times, our brain literally
forgets how to rest.

> Our mind needs
> time and space
> to catch up with
> what our soul
> already knows.

That's exactly what happened to me last February when
I decided to give up social media for Lent. For the first two
weeks, I found myself reaching for my phone every time I had
more than a few seconds of spare time. It was almost like my
hand simply needed to be holding my phone for my body to
feel whole. The phone had become an extension of my physical self; without it, I felt like a piece of me was missing. More
than a dozen times a day I picked up my phone, realized I had
nothing to check, stared at the screen for a second, and then
put the phone back down on the counter. I was astonished
by how restless I felt when I couldn't check email or scroll
through Instagram while standing in line at the grocery store
or while waiting in the car to pick up my kids from school.

Part of the reason I gravitated toward my phone was habit.
That neural pathway was so firmly cemented in my brain,
my hand performed the action of reaching for my phone

almost automatically, before I even realized what I was doing. But part of my inability to simply sit still and quiet in the in-between times was my relentless drive toward efficiency and productivity. I wanted to make good use of my time, and staring out the windshield into a gray winter afternoon seemed like a phenomenal waste.

This is also exactly why I was aghast at my son's lack of reading material as we sat on the shore of Lake Superior that chilly summer afternoon. There I was, in one of the most scenic spots in all of America, the lake water lapping at my feet, seagulls circling the sky, the jagged edge of the Sawtooth range in the distance, and I was bent on finishing a chapter in the book I was reading and moving on to the next. Busy was what my brain was used to, so busy I was going to be, regardless of my surroundings. I didn't give myself the opportunity to enter into directed rest that day, but even if I'd tried, I likely would have struggled to settle into a contemplative state simply because my brain was out of practice. I hadn't offered my brain a Sabbath in years.

Noah, on the other hand, was content to sit quietly, his face turned toward the vast expanse of water that stretched as far as the eye could see. I don't know what he thought about that afternoon as we sat side by side on the shore of Lake Superior. But I couldn't help but notice he was happy to do nothing. Unlike me, my son was simply content to be.

## GOING DEEPER

You may not be as prone to hustle as I am, but chances are, you too feel pressure to do, produce, and achieve from time to time. You too hear and heed society's demand to "make it happen." The truth is, though, just like a gardener cannot know a tree without examining it from every angle, we cannot know ourselves unless we explore both our exterior and interior terrain, a process that requires time, stillness, and space. We cannot begin to know ourselves until we allow silence and solitude into our lives.

Before you move on to the next chapter, it may be helpful for you to consider what circumstances, if any, propel you into hustle mode. Feel free to pen your thoughts in the space provided after each of the following questions. Or consider dedicating a special notebook or journal to this journey toward uncovering the true you.

Some questions to think about:

1. Are there times during which you are more prone to busyness? If so, how could you balance that busyness with periods of directed rest?

2. Are there certain circumstances or environments in which you are more apt to hustle? If so, how might you carve out opportunities for silence and stillness even amid these circumstances?

3. Do you ever find yourself pinning on the "badge of busyness" among particular friends, colleagues, or family members? If so, what might be behind that tendency?

4. What could be inhibiting you from engaging in regular periods of directed rest?

Take a moment to think about what you would need to establish a regular practice of directed rest. For instance, can you look at your daily schedule to identify the times in which you have a few spare minutes? Can you think of a spot that would be conducive to sitting in silence and stillness, even if only for five minutes? (For tips on how to begin a practice of directed rest, please see the appendix on pages 223–25.)

This week, try to carve out some time and space to quiet yourself. You might begin with just five minutes a day, as I did, or perhaps you have the opportunity for a longer respite. Whatever your circumstances, create a sliver of space in which you begin to become familiar with yourself, as a gardener becomes familiar with a tree.

# 2

# beneath the canopy

## Hearing what's been there all along

Our life becomes a series of choices between the fiction of our false-self, whom we feed with the illusions of passion and selfish appetite, and our true identity in the peace of God.

—Thomas Merton, *Seeds of Contemplation*

On a warm, rainy evening in August 1952, in a simple concert hall at the end of a dirt road near Woodstock, New York, an audience comprising mostly artists and members of New York City's classical music community gathered for a performance. Pianist David Tudor sat down on the piano bench, arranged his sheet music, and prepared to play a brand-new piece by composer John Cage.

But then Tudor did something unexpected. Instead of placing his fingers on the keys, he closed the lid of the piano, and, picking up a stopwatch, clicked the start button. Laying the stopwatch on the piano lid, Tudor sat quietly with his hands in his lap, occasionally turning a page of the music. After 30 seconds of silence, Tudor clicked the stopwatch off and opened the lid of the piano. Then, after a moment, he closed the lid and started the stopwatch again to time another 2 minutes, 23 seconds of silence. Tudor repeated the routine a third and final time, timing another 1 minute, 40 seconds of silence, before clicking the stopwatch off and gathering his music. He exited the stage, having never played a single note.

The audience was incensed. Midway through the second movement, restless throat clearing, coughing, and rustling could be heard over the staccato of rain on the roof of the concert hall. By the third movement of Tudor's performance, several members of the audience stormed out of the venue in a flurry of disgust. Tudor remembered one local community member exclaiming, during the post-concert discussion, "Good people of Woodstock, we should run these people out of town."[1]

The performance and the composition itself were not a joke. John Cage claimed 4′33″, as the piece came to be known for its duration of four minutes and thirty-three seconds, was his favorite and best work of all his compositions. "They missed the point," he insisted about the audience in Woodstock that night. "What they thought was silence, because they didn't know how to listen, was full of accidental sounds. You could hear the wind stirring outside during the first movement. During the second, raindrops began pattering on the roof, and during the third the people themselves made all kinds of interesting sounds as they talked or walked out."[2]

Cage said *4'33"* was inspired by the "white paintings" of Robert Rauschenberg, who created monochromatic works that, at least at first glance, look like nothing more than blank canvases. Cage, however, noted that a closer inspection of the paintings revealed an infinite variety of nuances—shadows, reflections, and variations created by dust particles. He was also influenced by an experience he'd had in an anechoic chamber at Harvard University, a room specially designed to maintain absolute silence for acoustic testing. When he stood in the room, Cage heard two sounds, one a higher pitch than the other. An engineer explained that what Cage was hearing was actually his own body—the higher-pitched sound was that of his nervous system, and the lower pitch was the sound of his blood circulating. That was the moment Cage realized there was no such thing as true silence, only the matter of not listening.

Having watched a performance of *4'33"* on YouTube, I understand why the audience was infuriated the evening of the debut in Woodstock. I can't imagine paying good money for concert tickets, only to witness a musician click a stopwatch on and off three times. The whole concept *is* a little absurd, especially if you are expecting actual music—or at least music in the traditional sense.

But here's something else I noticed when I watched the performance of Cage's silent composition: it was uncomfortable. Even though I was in the privacy of my own home, alone on my sofa with my computer on my lap, I found myself shifting uneasily as I watched the pianist sit in front of the keys and click a stopwatch. Part of me wanted to laugh and roll my eyes—*music . . . pshaw!* But part of me felt anxious, edgy, almost like I was watching something I wasn't supposed to. I fought the urge to close YouTube and shut my laptop. I fought the urge to walk away.

## What Lies Beneath

One early spring afternoon, a few months after I had begun the practice of sitting for five minutes a day (a practice that, by the way, Dr. Leaf would call directed rest), I sat on the park bench with Josie at my feet. As I rested in the quiet of the afternoon, I noticed the cool air on my face and the faint breeze in my hair. I saw that the leaves were just beginning to unfurl. The ravine sparkled with fresh, vibrant green, like a leprechaun had danced through the valley during the night, leaving a carpet of shamrock and jade in his wake.

While I'd grown used to the routine and had come to relish the few minutes of quiet, until that afternoon, not much had transpired during my five-minute respites. In the four months of near-daily sitting, I hadn't experienced any compelling revelations or especially deep thoughts. As I sat on the bench I typically let my mind wander, and mostly, it meandered toward the trivial and the mundane: what to write for the next day's blog post; what I should make for the teacher appreciation supper; if I'd remembered to switch the laundry from the washer to the dryer. Occasionally, especially when I tried to focus specifically on my breathing, I experienced a few brief moments in which the tumble of thoughts ceased and my mind felt suspended in a state of emptiness. Most days, though, as my brain skipped over random thoughts,

I passed the five minutes by watching the birds—the tiny nuthatches that skittered up and down the rough bark of the honey locust trees; the red-bellied woodpecker searching for insects with a rhythmic rap of his beak; the red-tailed hawk circling the sky above my head. I rarely looked at my phone to check the time anymore. When it felt right, I simply stood up and continued on.

That day, though, when I stood to step back onto the path, Josie tugging at the leash, a question quietly presented itself in my mind, apparently, inexplicably, out of nowhere:

*Why do you have trouble with intimacy?*

The query, a can-of-worms question if there ever was one, stopped me short. Where had it come from? What had prompted it? What did it mean? I didn't understand it, it didn't make sense, and frankly, the question wasn't one I was interested in pursuing. At all. I didn't like the feeling of uneasiness it churned up in the pit of my stomach.

*I don't have trouble with intimacy,* I thought. *My relationships are fine. Everything is fine. I'm plenty intimate. What in the world?*

This is what happens when we offer ourselves a "Sabbath for the brain." "When our brain enters the rest circuit," Dr. Leaf explains, "we don't actually rest; we move into a highly intelligent, self-reflective, directed state. And the more often we go there, the more we get in touch with the deep, spiritual part of who we are."[3] In quieting ourselves, we allow what lies beneath our everyday, ordinary thought processes

> In quieting ourselves, we allow what lies below our everyday, ordinary thought processes to begin to rise to the surface. We begin to hear what's been there all along.

to begin to rise to the surface. We begin to hear what's been there all along.

## Get to Know the Tree

Resting in this self-reflective state is the first step in pruning open—both in actual gardening as well as in the spiritual practice of pruning. Before a gardener even picks up the pruning shears, her first job is to observe the tree, becoming familiar with how it looks from all angles and how it behaves in every season. Garden designer Judy Maier also suggests that the gardener try to piece together the tree's history in order to understand what it needs now and what it might need in the future, as well as the circumstances of its planting and the elements that have affected it over time. Some gardeners begin the pruning process not with shears or a saw but with a pencil and paper, sketching the tree as it looks in its present form and how they imagine it might look after pruning.[4]

In other words, deep transformation, in both the garden and in ourselves, requires observation, reflection, and time. The problem is, we rarely allow ourselves the opportunity to enter into the thoughtful, observant state of rest required for this metaphorical archaeology because we are afraid of what it could reveal. In my case, I didn't want anything to do with the startling, unsettling question about intimacy that suddenly rose to the surface during my quiet contemplation. I didn't want to peer under the canopy of my cozy, self-protective layers and into the stark—perhaps ugly—reality that lay underneath.

And so, as quickly as that uncomfortable question about intimacy bubbled to the surface, I squashed it. I squeezed it back into my subconscious and let the leaves and branches swing back into place. It was easy for me to ignore what I had glimpsed under the canopy, to allow the distractions and busyness of my life to sweep it away, to get on with deadlines and dinner and walking the dog. Less than ten seconds after the question about intimacy had reverberated in my head, I had already forgotten it. A mere ten steps from the bench, my brain was already focused on something else.

Deep transformation, in both the garden and in ourselves, requires observation, reflection, and time. The problem is, we rarely allow ourselves the opportunity to enter into the thoughtful, observant state of rest required for this metaphorical archaeology because we are afraid of what it could reveal.

I wouldn't realize it until many months later, but that question about intimacy was one to listen to. That one small, unnerving question had risen from the depths of my soul, from the desires of my deepest self. The question was critically important, but as quickly as I could, I buried it beneath the detritus of my daily life.

I wonder if this is what happened to some of the audience members as they sat in the concert hall at the debut of *4′33″* that night. Part of their irritation was surely spurred by the fact that they felt duped. They'd paid for a ticket to hear music, not silence or random noises, after all. But I also suspect that beneath that irritation and sense of betrayal was anxiety, discomfort, and perhaps even fear. Unaccustomed to silence and to being alone with their own thoughts for even a few short minutes, many of the audience members rebelled. They fled. They simply could not bear the quiet. Or perhaps more to the point: they could not bear to listen to what the quiet revealed.

Cultural standards for busyness and an addiction to busyness are indeed real. But I also believe there is something deeper and more insidious behind our propensity for relentless activity. I suspect many of us use it as a way to avoid what simmers beneath the surface of our consciousness. We use busyness and productivity both consciously and subconsciously as our metaphorical branches and leaves—layers of protection between us and our own souls. The busier and more productive we are, the less likely we'll have the time or inclination to dig deep beneath our self-protective covering. And in those rare moments when we do allow ourselves a respite in silence and solitude, we often react like the audience members at the Cage concert did, and like I did that spring afternoon on the park bench. We are restless, agitated, defensive, and perhaps even a little angry. And our inclination is to storm out of the concert hall or away from the park bench. Our inclination is to flee.

Busyness allows us to avoid the deepest questions of our souls. It keeps us at arm's length from our truest, most authentic selves. And when we don't know our deepest, most authentic selves, we can't know what work and what role God has for us in this world. In fact, when we don't know our deepest, most authentic selves, we don't really know God, because it is God who creates our innermost selves, and it's God who invites this authentic self into deep relationship with him.

Author and spiritual director Ruth Haley Barton puts it like this: "The willingness to see ourselves as we are and name it in God's presence is at the very heart of the spiritual journey."[5] Too often, though, we simply refuse to do the hard, intimidating work of quieting ourselves—the listening, waiting, and observing that is required for spiritual transformation. We would rather check another item off the to-do list, squeeze in another errand, queue up another podcast, binge-watch another six episodes of our favorite Netflix series—anything so as not to confront our truest selves, our most pressing fears, and our deepest desires.

My own experience is proof positive that if you stick with it long enough and consistently enough, even five minutes will offer a sliver of opportunity for the deepest desires of your soul to emerge bit by bit, one question, thought, or insight at a time. The question about intimacy that bubbled to the surface the day I stood up from the park bench wasn't a fluke. The fact that it presented itself right then was the result of consistently practicing quiet, stillness, and contemplation over a period of months. In brief stints of five minutes at a time, I had trained my brain to switch into directed rest, and over time, that space and time began to reveal the deepest desires of my soul.

## The Soul Is Like a Wild Animal

Many years ago, my husband and I embarked on a backpacking trip in Glacier National Park. Because of the prevalence of grizzly bears throughout the region, we were required to watch a video about wilderness safety before we departed.

In addition to suggesting that we strap a canister of pepper spray to our belt loops, the ranger on duty also instructed us to make a lot of noise while we were hiking. The last thing we wanted to do in the backcountry was startle a grizzly bear, especially a mama grizzly with cubs, he cautioned. However, the ranger assured us, if bears were aware of approaching humans in advance, they usually headed in the opposite direction.

Brad and I took the ranger's advice seriously. We made as much racket as possible, clapping our hands, whistling, and yelling, "Hey, bear! Hey there, bear!" every few minutes during the several hours it took to hike to our campsite. Obviously, it was not the most peaceful hiking experience. Plus, not only did we not see a grizzly bear, we also scared away every deer, raccoon, squirrel, chipmunk, rabbit, and bird for miles. There we were, in the middle of one of the most pristine wildernesses in the world, and we didn't see a single species of wildlife for the entire two days.

I thought about that noisy backpacking trip recently when I read what Parker Palmer says about the soul:

> The soul is like a wild animal—tough, resilient, savvy, self-sufficient, and yet exceedingly shy. If we want to see a wild animal, the last thing we should do is to go crashing through the woods, shouting for the creature to come out. But if we are willing to walk quietly into the woods and sit silently for an hour or two at the base of a tree, the creature we are waiting for may well emerge, and out of the corner of an eye we will catch a glimpse of the precious wildness we seek.[6]

In other words, the soul is like a grizzly bear in the wild. If you want to avoid it, keep crashing around and making as much noise as possible. But if you want to catch a glimpse of the soul's "precious wildness," you must get quiet. Regular periods of quiet and solitude for an hour or two are ideal, as Palmer observes. On the other hand, you have to start somewhere, and five minutes is better than nothing.

Once you begin to glimpse the "precious wildness" you seek, once you begin to hear the questions and the first inkling of your soul's deepest desires, the key, of course, is to keep listening with courage and self-compassion, to keep sitting quietly "in the stark, fragile reality of you," as author Adam McHugh says in his book *The Listening Life*.[7] As my own startled reaction to the unexpected question about intimacy indicates, and as McHugh implies here, listening to your own soul is harder than you might expect. As you begin to hear these early murmurings of your soul, your inclination may be to turn away, to stuff the uncomfortable thought or question that's risen to the surface back into the depths of your subconscious, to run out of the concert hall, so to speak. That's what I did. I turned away from that question about intimacy; I ignored it. Yet it wasn't gone for good. Though I'd tried to quell the question, I didn't eliminate it entirely. It simply lurked beneath the surface, waiting for another opportune moment to present itself.

## Why We Avoid the Now

I remember a conversation I had at the beginning of the school year with my then eleven-year-old son, Rowan. We were lying in his bed, light from the hallway falling in a rectangle over the tangle of blankets. He was turned away from me, his face toward the window, his voice small, muffled by the pillow. "My life is going by too fast," he said.

Already Rowan was feeling and experiencing the passage of time, the ephemerality of life. His first year of middle school was a period of transition as he began to step from young childhood toward adulthood, and he was resisting. I heard regret in his voice as he spoke wistfully about days gone by—toys he'd outgrown, books that were now too "babyish." "I want to slow it down," he whispered to me.

That night as I lay next to him, I told Rowan what I always tell him when we have these conversations, which is that the key to slowing down is to live more fully in the present moment. My son, like me, tends to live ahead, mind and heart fixed on what's next—the next assignment, the next item on the to-do list, the next vacation, the next goal, the next fun thing—instead of what's here right now. In fact, just recently, Rowan told my husband and me that his life philosophy is, "It can always be better"—as in, "This is good, but I bet there's something better around the corner." Honestly, I can relate. Like the commuters who streamed by Joshua Bell in the metro station, too busy to stop for beauty, overpowered by the surge of everyday life, Rowan and I are constantly moving forward, our eyes eagerly looking for what's beyond the bend, rather than what's right in front of us.

I am, rather desperately at times, attempting to retrain my own brain while I try to help Rowan cement positive neural pathways in his. "Be aware of the present moment, the experience that's happening right now," I whispered to my son the night we lay side by side in his twin bed. "Live the now instead of the 'what's next,' and you'll live more slowly and more fully." Rowan didn't respond to my advice.

I'm not sure he was listening to me. I'm not sure I was listening to myself.

I think back often to that bedtime conversation with Rowan. I urged him to live in the present moment, to live what I called a "right-now life," to "awaken to the holiness of life" (1 Cor. 15:34 Message), though I didn't use those exact words. I suggested that to slow the relentless drumbeat of time, he need only slow his own rhythms, to focus on today, on the present moment rather than on yesterday or tomorrow. What I was advising my son, essentially, was that he needed to allow space and time for a "Sabbath in the brain": space and time for directed rest.

I realize now, of course, that my advice was easier to offer than it is to heed, because to slow to the present moment is to take stock of now, and the "now" we experience isn't always what we expect or hope it will be. Frankly, the "now" isn't always a delightfully unexpected Joshua Bell concert. More often, the "now" is the performance of the John Cage composition: unnerving, uncomfortable, perhaps slightly weird. Often the "now" holds questions, uncertainty, and disappointment, or even hopelessness and despair, fear and brokenness. Sometimes the "now" holds everything we would rather avoid.

So that's what we do. We avoid. We busy ourselves to avoid. Like the oak tree in my backyard, we sprout leaf after leaf after leaf—more projects, more responsibilities, more chores, more clutter, more hustle, more activities, more fun, more books, more Netflix, more to-do lists—until we are full to bursting. The irony is that all that busyness and productivity looks beautiful and fulfilling, at least initially and at least from the outside. These are not dead branches I'm talking about here. Instead, we are like the summer oak tree, dense with lush foliage, our branches heavy with the abundance of all we have acquired, accomplished, and produced.

But the reality is that underneath those many, many leaves, we are straining beneath the weight. It's crowded in there. Eventually, as we add more and more, there's less and less light, less and less room to grow. Until finally, clinging tighter than ever to our many branches and leaves . . . we break.

## GOING DEEPER

Like me, you may be unaccustomed to sitting quietly and contemplatively for even five or ten minutes at a time. Know that it's okay to feel uncomfortable or uneasy as you sit during your periods of directed rest. Try not to force the process. It may take minutes, it may take months, but eventually the deepest desires of your soul will begin to surface.

Here are a few questions to consider as you begin to dip into short periods of directed rest (for specific, practical tips on establishing a regular practice of directed rest, see the appendix on pages 223–25):

1. How do you feel as you sit quietly in silence? What emotions are you experiencing? These feelings and emotions may range from a sense of peacefulness and fulfillment to unease, anxiety, fear, and even anger. Try to acknowledge your emotions and make space for them without necessarily analyzing them.

2. Do you discern any new or unexpected questions or thoughts bubbling to the surface? If so, can you acknowledge these thoughts or questions, rather than automatically pressing them back down into your subconscious?

3. What are some of the "leaves and branches" on your "tree" that may be distracting you and keeping you at arm's length from the deepest desires of your soul? Are there certain times or circumstances in your life that cause you to add more and more leaves and branches?

4. Are you like my son Rowan and me, focused on the "what's next" instead of the right now? How can you work toward living more in the present moment?

# 3

# broken limbs

## Do you want to get well?

Pain demands to be felt—or it will demand you feel nothing at all.

—Ann Voskamp, *The Broken Way*

It began with a dull but persistent ache in my left elbow. At first I couldn't figure out how I'd injured it. I don't lift weights or play golf or tennis. I didn't recall banging my arm hard on a door frame or straining the muscle by lifting something especially heavy. The only activity I could link to the pain was a session of vigorous backyard pruning I'd engaged in a few weeks back. But it couldn't possibly be that, I assumed. After all, who gets injured pruning shrubbery?

Ever since we'd returned from Portland, I hadn't been able to stop thinking about the Japanese garden we'd toured. I yearned for the openness and space, the feeling of lightness and airiness I'd experienced there. Yet when I stood on my patio and gazed into my own backyard, all I saw was a tangled thicket of spirea and barberry shrubs, overgrown lilac and burning bushes, a tired crab apple, a gangly river birch, and a magnolia stuffed into a cramped space next to the house. In short, what I wanted in my backyard was an oasis of spacious tranquility; what I had was an overrun mess.

I knew nothing about the Japanese art of aesthetic pruning. Nevertheless, armed with a single piece of knowledge (that fall is generally a good time to prune trees and shrubs) and a pair of dull clippers I'd grabbed from the hook in the garage, I donned my husband's oversized work gloves, pushed my hair into a headband, and strode toward the two shrubs that pressed up against the sunroom windows.

I worked on those two bushes most of the morning, clipping a branch here and a twig there, stepping back to survey my work and then plunging into the thicket again, each time removing a little more of the foliage in my quest to prune open the center of the shrubs. Some of the branches were quite thick, and as I strained to clamp the metal blade of my loppers around the tough wood, slicing through green sinuous fibers, squeezing the long handles together with all my strength, I felt muscles I didn't even know I had begin to quiver and burn.

Two hours later, a pile of clipped branches and wilted leaves at my feet, my arms scratched bloody, sweat beading my brow, I stood back, pleased with my work. With much of the foliage and all of the deadwood removed, the shrubs' main branches were now discernible, arching elegantly away from the sunroom windows. Late afternoon light dappled the shade underneath, and a gentle breeze fluttered the scarlet leaves. The rest of my yard was still an overgrown mess, but these two bushes, at least, were now properly pruned. Abandoning the pile of branches and twigs to bag up later, I moved on to the spirea that lined the picket fence. I couldn't wait to tackle the rest of the yard.

By the end of the weekend, I had eighteen paper leaf bags and four plastic barrels stuffed with leaves, branches, and even a couple of small limbs to show for my work. My yard, in my opinion, looked vastly improved—tidier, airier, more open, and markedly less brambly. My son Noah, on the other hand, was horrified. "Nice job, Paul Bunyan," he remarked, standing on the back patio with his arms crossed. Apparently he preferred a less manicured look.

Pleased as I was with my newfound landscaping skills, I was also very, very sore. Turns out, pruning is hard work. My quads and hamstrings were sore from all the bending and crouching; my shoulders, neck, and lower back were stiff; and strangely, I noticed, my left elbow ached and was tender to the touch. That Sunday night, I popped a couple ibuprofen, cranked the heating pad to high, settled into the sofa, and didn't give my aches and pains another thought.

Three months later, however, my left elbow still throbbed. In fact, it was much, much worse. Each night when I slid under the covers I carefully cushioned my arm with multiple pillows, nestling it up against my rib cage. Most nights, though, this elaborate ritual was futile; the aching was so bad it often awakened me from sleep. I couldn't lift the teakettle off the stove or the milk jug from the fridge. Twice a week

I asked my husband to haul the laundry hamper down two flights of stairs from our bedroom to the basement; it hurt my elbow too much to carry it myself. I was taking ibuprofen almost daily, though it barely dulled the persistent pain, and every evening I kept my arm wrapped in a heating pad while I watched TV.

"You really need to make an appointment with an orthopedist," my husband advised, after I'd complained about the discomfort for the umpteen millionth time. "That kind of relentless pain isn't normal."

"It's fine," I insisted. I told myself the discomfort would eventually go away on its own. My plan was to "wait and see." Deep down, though, I think I knew Brad was right. I think I knew that whatever was wrong with my elbow was beyond a simple muscle pull. I also suspected it wasn't going to get better on its own. Yet I resisted. I was in denial, refusing to admit my elbow was bad enough to see a doctor. Day after day, week after week, I procrastinated calling the orthopedist's office for an appointment. I didn't want to live with the debilitating pain that was clearly impacting my daily life, yet I also refused to pick up the phone and take the first step toward a remedy.

Of course I did what we all do when we are suffering from a physical malady: I googled my symptoms. WebMD informed me that I likely had one of two problems. Best-case scenario: tendonitis (otherwise known as "tennis elbow"—or in my case, "pruning elbow"). Worst-case scenario: a torn tendon. Tendonitis, I learned, is typically treated with a combination of physical therapy and cortisone injections, while a torn tendon is remedied with surgery. Neither option was particularly appealing. Who has time for weekly physical therapy sessions? Who in their right mind wants a needle the size of a yardstick (I'm exaggerating . . . but barely) inserted into their tender, aching elbow? Who wants surgery, with anesthesia and scalpels and more pain? Not me, that's who.

The truth is, I was afraid of surgery. I'd never had more than a couple of stitches, never broken a bone, never been under anesthesia. I was afraid of the pain, and worse, I was afraid of surrendering my body to another human being, a stranger. What if the surgeon made the injury worse? What if he or she made a mistake? What if something went wrong? It sounds silly, I realize. After all, we're talking outpatient elbow surgery, not a quadruple bypass. But as ridiculous as it sounds, it's the truth: I was afraid, and because of that fear, I resisted making the call. Rather than taking the frightening but ultimately healing step toward diagnosis and treatment, I chose to live with the familiar and therefore less threatening pain of what had become a debilitating, chronic condition.

## Do You Want to Get Well?

One day, while Jesus was visiting Jerusalem for Passover, he walked by a pool where the sick and disabled gathered in the shade. Legend had it that an angel of the Lord would descend to stir the waters from time to time, and the first person who entered the pool when its waters were disturbed would be cured of whatever affliction he or she suffered. Dozens of ill and disabled people waited by the pool each day, hoping for a chance to be the first person to enter the rippling water, hoping for a chance to be healed.

Jesus came upon a man lying near the water who had been ill for thirty-eight years. Turning to the man, Jesus asked him what sounded like a simple question: "Do you want to get well?" (John 5:6). Every time I read this story, Jesus' question always sounds odd to me. After all, the man had made his way down to the healing pool every day for decades, hoping that somehow, someday, he would be the first to touch the water when it was stirred by the angel. It seems obvious the man wanted to be well. Why else would he go to the trouble of hauling himself there day after day? The man himself told Jesus as much. The problem was, he explained, he hadn't been healed because someone always managed to slip into the pool first. Since he was too ill (or perhaps paralyzed, as some Bible translations state) to walk himself, and since he didn't have anyone to carry him, the man was never able to make it to the water in time to be healed.

We don't know much about the man lying next to the pool of Bethesda. Aside from the fact that he'd been ill or disabled for thirty-eight years, that he'd been coming to the pool for healing, presumably for a long time, and that so far, he'd been unable to reach the waters, we don't hear anything else about his daily existence. Yet even these sparse details are enough for us to understand the deeper implication behind Jesus' puzzling question: *Do you want to get well?* What appears at first glance an odd, unnecessary question with an obvious answer is, in reality, much more complicated.

Thirty-eight years is a long time. It's more than enough time for a person to settle into a daily routine, to establish habits and practices that will enable survival. It's probably enough time for a person to get used to a situation, in spite of the challenges inherent in those circumstances. Thirty-eight years is enough time to grow complacent. It's enough time to become resigned. Thirty-eight years is enough time to become leery of any proposed alternative, especially one that sounds too good to be true.

Think about the man's situation for a moment. Likely unable to work, he undoubtedly received handouts of food, drink, and money from people passing by the pool. He had almost certainly established routines that allowed him to receive assistance and benefit from the generosity of others. After thirty-eight years of living on the streets of Jerusalem, the man knew what he had to do to survive. After thirty-eight years, his daily routine was ingrained in him. He'd been sick for so long—perhaps for his entire life—he could hardly remember any other way. While his life was likely not easy, at the very least it was familiar. After thirty-eight years, being sick and dependent on others was the only life the man knew.

The self-created identity of the man at the pool of Bethesda was "sick." "A sick man" was who he was and how he had defined himself for thirty-eight years. This was not his core identity—his "soul, [his] True Self, [his] unique blueprint"[1]— the identity given to him by God when God wove him together. "A sick man" was the identity he had adopted after years of illness and dysfunction. His habits and routines, his entire way of life, in fact, supported that identity. His life revolved around his sickness. The ill man's daily routines and habits, such as sitting by the pool, passing the time, waiting for someone to carry him to the healing waters, were the scaffolding that supported his self-created false identity. The status quo—the familiar—was easy. Stepping into wellness— the unknown—was a risk.

Jesus stood before the man and offered him the hope of real healing and a transformed life. To be truly well was probably not a reality the man had considered for a long time, if ever. And yet here the gift of healing was being extended like a cool cup of water in the midst of a desert. It was decision time. All that was required of the man was the faith and trust to say yes to Jesus' question.

I wonder if, in that moment, the man had doubts. I wonder if he was skeptical of Jesus' invitation. After all, it sounded a little too easy, after thirty-eight years spent languishing at the pool, to simply stand as Jesus had instructed. I wonder if the man was afraid to trust, afraid of being disappointed or let down. I wonder, too, if he considered how answering yes to Jesus' question and standing to walk would impact his life—how, as a healed man, he would be expected to find work, to forgo the assistance of others and learn to provide for himself instead. Did he consider the new challenges healing would present? Was he afraid of the freedom that awaited him? I wonder if the man had ever really, truly considered what it would mean for him to be well.

## Sometimes We Don't Recognize When We Are Sick

Change—even good, transforming, healing change—is hard. We develop habits and routines for ourselves that offer comfort in their familiarity. We are set in our ways, unwilling to give up the false securities and identities we've crafted as self-protection. We are unwilling to trust, unwilling to surrender. As Franciscan priest Richard Rohr says, "Setting out is always a leap of faith, a risk in the deepest sense of the term. . . . The familiar and the habitual are so falsely reassuring, most of us make our homes there permanently."[2] I know this firsthand because I've experienced it, not only when I injured my elbow and refused to call the doctor, but also in my life as a whole.

Like the man lying beside the pool, I didn't recognize the false identity I'd crafted for myself over the years. My self-created identity was "producer" and "achiever." This was not the identity God gave me when he wove me together; this was the identity I created for myself and then pursued as if my life depended on it. My daily routines and habits—busyness, efficiency, production, ticking off boxes on a never-ending to-do list—were the scaffolding that supported my self-created identity. My false identity was really the only identity I'd ever known or recognized, and it was so familiar, so routine, so second-nature, I never entertained the possibility of any other option.

The question about intimacy I heard that day on the park bench was an important one because it was a question from God. I know this now, although I didn't realize it at the time. That weird, unexpected, uncomfortable question was essentially Jesus' way of asking me, "Do you want to be well?" In other words, "Do you want to drop your self-created identity and embrace the person I created you to be?"

In that moment, I was the sick man lying next to the pool of Bethesda. But unlike the sick man, I didn't even acknowledge the question I was being asked because I didn't recognize I was sick. In fact, I'm sure God had asked me this same question numerous times before in various iterations, but until that day on the park bench, I'd never even heard it. And here's the most important point: I'd never heard the question because I'd always been too busy to stop and listen for it. I couldn't hear the invitation into healing through the cacophony of my own clanging, hustle-produce-achieve-succeed life. Unlike the man at the pool, I wasn't ever still enough to hear the question Jesus yearned for me to answer. I was so busy maintaining the scaffolding that was keeping my self-created identity intact, I didn't have the time or space to listen to much else.

That day on the park bench, however, I was still. After weeks of daily sitting, I was finally learning to be quiet, at least for a few minutes at a time. And in that quiet space, in that small window of silence and solitude, God slipped in with an invitation. He'd undoubtedly been inviting me all along.

As author Mark Buchanan points out, God often speaks in questions. He does so in the Bible (think, for example, about one of the first communications between God and human beings, when God asks Adam and Eve in the garden, after they've eaten the fruit, "Where are you?" [Gen. 3:9]), and he does so in our own present-day lives. "What does the Voice speak?" Buchanan asks. "More often than not, a question."[3]

When I heard the question about intimacy that day on the park bench, I didn't immediately recognize the voice as God's. In fact, it actually sounded a lot like my own voice, in my own head. Dallas Willard says this is the way God most often speaks to us—"in our own spirits." Willard adds, "The form of one's own thoughts and attendant feelings is the most common path for hearing God for those who are living in harmony with God. God uses our self-knowledge or self-awareness to search us out and reveal to us the truth about ourselves and our world."[4] The question about intimacy wasn't so much a question from myself to myself, but from God to me. Disconcerting though it was, the question was an invitation into wellness and wholeness—an invitation to name my sickness, to acknowledge it, and to begin the journey toward discovering my truest, most authentic self, the God-created self hidden beneath the false identity I'd clung to for so long.

But unlike the man at Bethesda, I didn't answer God's question. I didn't say yes to the invitation. Leery and a little afraid of what lay beyond the invitation and beneath that unnerving question, I shut it down as quickly as possible and resumed my breakneck production schedule. No time for questions like that when there's a dog to walk and emails to answer and a Tupperware drawer to organize!

That day on the park bench I did not stand up and step into vulnerability and exposure. Instead, I stayed right where I was, stagnating at the edge of the pool. I stayed in the place I knew, where familiarity and routine reigned. I refused to relinquish what I'd built and what I thought I knew for the mystery God was inviting me into. As Rohr acknowledges, "If you have spent many years building your particular tower of success and self-importance—your personal 'salvation project,' as Thomas Merton called it—you won't want to leave it."[5] I didn't want to abandon the identity I'd created and all the routines and habits holding that identity in place. I turned down the invitation into true wholeness and wellness. The truth is, I wouldn't even admit I was sick.

## Wilt Thou Be Made Whole?

Eight months after Prune-a-palooza, I finally called and made an appointment with an orthopedist. In the exam room, after he had bent my elbow back and forth and pressed and prodded and moved it this way and that, the doctor asked me when I had first noticed the pain. "It's been a while," I answered, unwilling to admit the injury was several months old.

The doctor pressed for more information: "How long is a while? Two weeks? A month? Two months?"

"Well . . ." I hesitated. "More like eight months."

The orthopedist stopped typing and looked up from his computer screen. "What took you so long to come in?" he asked, meeting my eyes over the laptop.

"I don't know." I shrugged. "I guess I was hoping it would get better on its own."

The truth is, I'd been in denial for much of those eight months, refusing to acknowledge there was a real problem behind the pain in my elbow. I didn't want to admit there was something truly wrong, and so I told myself, and my husband, that it was "fine." I ignored the obvious symptoms because I was afraid and frankly because I didn't want to deal with the hassle of doctor's appointments and physical therapy and treatments and possible surgery. In some ways, it seemed easier and less painful to stay broken than it was to be healed.

In the end, I needed physical therapy and multiple injections administered with a needle that looked better suited for knitting than cortisone delivery. And when those remedies failed, I ended up having surgery for what an MRI ultimately revealed to be a torn tendon. Recovery was even more painful and more tedious than I'd feared. Suffice it to say, wearing a cast in Nebraska's searing August heat is nothing short of the itchiest form of torture you can imagine. Eight months later, however, I can state with confidence that my elbow is as good as new (albeit with the addition of a glamorous two-inch scar). Last weekend I even pruned a couple of shrubs for the first time since the initial injury, though I was markedly less ambitious this time.

The journey to wholeness and healing, it turns out, does not begin with surgery or even with diagnosis. The journey to wholeness begins with admitting you are broken. That's why Jesus asked the man at the pool of Bethesda, "Do you want to get well?" Or, as the King James translation so tellingly puts it: "Wilt thou be made whole?"

When I read that question aloud, I always put the emphasis on the word "want" (or, in King James, "wilt"), because to me, it's a question about desire—"Do you *want* to get well?" "*Wilt* thou be made whole?" Wellness—wholeness—is a choice given to us. Jesus knows true wholeness requires more than the act of healing itself. The journey to true wholeness requires our desire to be well, our desire to be whole. And our desire to be well and whole grows first out of an acknowledgment that we are broken.

> The journey to wholeness and healing, it turns out, does not begin with surgery or even with diagnosis. The journey to wholeness begins with admitting you are broken.

Jesus' question, "Do you want to get well?" clearly sparked something deep within the man at the pool, igniting a desire that overpowered his doubts and fears and propelled him to step beyond his familiar routine. As Ruth Haley Barton observes in *Sacred Rhythms*, "The man reached within himself to that place of deep desire and deep faith and did what he was told. Somehow his willingness to follow his desire opened the way for him to experience Jesus' healing power."[6] His choice to stand when Jesus commanded him to was an act of faith. The man was healed, but he had to stand in faith, putting his trust in Jesus, in order to reveal the healing.

Sometimes, it seems, God heals without any participation or collaboration from us. Other times, perhaps more often, God invites us into the healing he is doing in us. We do not need to heal ourselves—the indwelling Holy Spirit does that for us—but we do need to *want* to get well; we need to desire wellness and choose it. And in order to want to get well, and ultimately to *be* well, we first have to acknowledge and name the problem that stands in the way.

My trouble—and perhaps you can relate—was that I had no sense whatsoever of my deepest desires. I had no idea what my soul longed for. If you'd asked me what my deepest desires were at the time the question about intimacy bubbled to the surface, my answer undoubtedly would have been connected to productivity or achievement. *To be a successful author. To sell more books. To have a bigger platform.* I know those answers sound shallow and empty, but that's the honest truth. I had no idea what I truly desired. I was chasing shallow wants that skittered over the surface. I was chasing the wind.

"When was the last time you felt it—your own longing, that is? Your longing for love, your longing for God, your longing to live your life as it is meant to be lived in God?" Barton asks in *Sacred Rhythms*. "When was the last time you felt a longing for healing and fundamental change groaning within you?"[7] I underlined those sentences the first time I read them, but I don't know that I really *read* them. I saw the words, but I didn't *see* them. "Do not rush past this question," Barton cautions; "it may be the most important question you ever ask."[8]

I rushed past the question. I'd been rushing past the question for my entire life—a life so crammed to overflowing, full with everything I thought I needed and everything I thought I desired. I was blind to my own emptiness, my own longing. I was fine. Everything was fine. I didn't have time for desires. I had no desires. I didn't feel "a longing for healing and fundamental change" because I didn't need to be healed or changed.

Or so I thought.

## Let Your Soul Speak

A tree will tell you when it's ill, broken, or in need of a good pruning, but the signs are often subtle—two branches crossed at an odd angle; bark that's cracked or that silently weeps fluid; discolored leaves; dark, brittle branches and twigs; fungal growth. Recently the 100-year-old pin oak in my backyard lost a large chunk of thick bark about a quarter of the way up its trunk. One day we noticed the bark looked loose and appeared to be pulling away from the rest of the tree. A few weeks later a two-foot section of bark plummeted to the ground, leaving a swath of bare, light-colored wood exposed on the trunk. It could be that the tree is simply going through a rapid growth spurt following a period of drought—outgrowing its bark like a snake outgrows its skin. On the other hand, the loss of bark may be an indication of pest infestation or the result of a fungal disease. Only a certified arborist will be able to definitely tell us what, if anything, afflicts the oak tree.

Similarly, the leaves of the river birch tree that abuts our backyard patio turn yellow and drop from its branches when the weather turns hot and dry. The first year this happened I called the local nursery in a panic, assuming the tree was dying. Turns out, river birches don't do well in drought, but there is an easy remedy. After a few days with a steadily dripping hose laid at the base of its trunk, the river birch perked up and our patio was no longer littered with prematurely yellow leaves.

Our own souls will tell us where we are broken and in need of healing, but like the trees in my backyard, the signs are often subtle—a crack or fissure; a brittleness; a fading or drooping; an unexpected weeping; a raw, exposed place. This is why quiet, stillness, silence, and solitude are so imperative. We need time, space, and stillness not only to observe what's happening on the surface, but also to discern what these subtle signs can tell us about what's going on deep within.

Turns out, I may not have outwardly acknowledged what needed healing in me, but my soul knew. My soul was working on a new thing deep inside me, before I was even aware of it. It's why I stopped to sit on the park bench. It's why I sat on that park bench every day for months on end, through the blistering heat of summer and the biting winds of winter. I didn't really get it at the time. I hardly knew why I was sitting there day in and day out. I thought I simply needed a little quiet, a break from the constant hum of my daily life. But my soul knew. My truest, most authentic self knew. The person deep inside me, the person created and woven together by God, knew and yearned for me to say yes to the invitation into wholeness.

It's tempting to rush past longing and desire. I know this, because rushing past was my modus operandi for as long as I can remember. But we must resist the temptation. Looking desire and longing in the eye is uncomfortable, I know. It's frightening and unnerving. But tapping into that deep desire—reaching down, like the man at the pool of Bethesda did, and being willing to name your desire—is the key to living into your God-given wholeness.

You have desire. Desire is inside you, and it's there even when you don't recognize it or acknowledge it. Desire is what compels us toward God. It's the Holy Spirit, thrumming and pulsating with life and love, propelling us forward, leading us by the hand toward a deep understanding of our belovedness. "Desire," Barton says, "is the life-blood surging through the heart of the spiritual life. You may not realize it, but your desire for God is the truest, most essential thing about you. Your desire for God and your capacity to connect with God as a human soul is the essence of who you are."[9]

Your soul will reveal your broken places, the wounded parts of you that need healing and restoration. Your soul will tell you how your life is meant to be lived in God and with God. Your soul will reveal your deepest longing. Your soul will speak. But first, you must be still enough to hear its quiet whisper.

## GOING DEEPER

Once again, it all comes back to stillness, space, and solitude. We must give ourselves the opportunity to be still in order to be present for God, to be quiet in order to hear the whispers of our soul. We cannot begin the process of healing until we first acknowledge that we are wounded, and that kind of deep, honest acknowledgment requires time, stillness, and space.

As you continue to sit for regular periods of directed rest, consider these questions:

1. Ask yourself the question Jesus presented to the man at the pool of Bethesda: "Do you *want* to get well?" If you find yourself resisting, can you examine the reasons why the question feels uncomfortable or even threatening? What might some of your reasons be for resisting wholeness and wellness? How could stepping into wellness be a risk for you? What might you have to give up to be well?

2. The false identity of the man at the pool was "a sick man." My self-created false identity was "producer" and "achiever." Can you identify a false identity you

have created for yourself? Give it a name. How have your habits and routines reinforced that false identity?

3. Can you allow your deepest desires to rise to the surface? Can you identify your longing, your deepest desire, or, like me, do you have trouble doing so? Write down longings and desires that come to mind. And if none do, think about that. Is it possible that you don't have longings and desires? Or do you need to give them more time and space to emerge?

4. Like a tree that offers subtle signs of inner wounds, is your body or soul offering you hints of wounds that need healing? Can you acknowledge those signs and then begin the process of uncovering what lies beneath them?

# 4

## seeds of desire

### Facing your deepest brokenness

God comes to me where I live and loves me where
I am. If I am not where I am, God cannot meet
me.

—Brennan Manning, *Souvenirs of Solitude*

Eyes watering with fatigue, I stumbled across the concrete,
the roar of the airplane engine fading into the background.
Inside the terminal, the crowd swirled around me. Every-
where there was chaos, movement, and noise—families embracing, young children crying, travelers wrenching suitcases
from the baggage conveyor, a cacophony of voices, a whirl-
wind of frenzied gesticulation. I smelled coffee, rich and
strong. Next to me a couple kissed long, like a scene from

a movie. All around me the air rang with words I could not understand.

I had arrived in Italy for a ten-day spiritual writers' retreat. For months, ever since I had mailed in my deposit, I had fretted over this trip. I realize this is more than a little ridiculous. After all, it's not like I was journeying to Botswana or Bangladesh: it was Italy, for heaven's sake—land of gelato and beautiful handcrafted leather goods. The truth is, though, I'm not much of a traveler. My favorite place in the world is my own backyard. The one and only time I had ever traveled overseas was twenty-four years prior, when I was in college and visited a friend in London, where, I feel compelled to remind you, they speak English. (And even then, when I sat next to a couple of Scots on the train to Edinburgh, I literally couldn't understand a word they said. I spent eight hours nodding and smiling awkwardly.)

I worried about every detail of this trip to Italy in the weeks and months leading up to my departure, from the language barrier to the long flight to the foreign currency. I know myself. My ability to do simple math vanishes under pressure. I panic when I have to make change in a New York City cab, inevitably undertipping or overtipping—and that's with American currency. *How will I figure out the euro? How will I pay the cab driver and the gelato seller?* I fretted in the middle of the night.

I'd jotted a dozen or so words and phrases in my journal and practiced pronouncing them over and over with Google translator—*grazie, bagno, buon giorno, per favore, bene*—but my inability to trill my *r*'s properly was a dead giveaway. Languages are not my forte. In high school I'd taken four years of Latin—a dead language . . . need

I say more? *What if I can't find my driver at the airport? How will I get to the hotel with my nonexistent Italian and math paralysis?*

And then there were the flights—one hour to Chicago, ten hours from Chicago to Munich, one hour from Munich to Florence. I am a notoriously anxious flyer, terrified of turbulence and germs and dying. The first thing I do upon boarding an airplane is to furiously scrub down the armrests, seatbelt buckle, and tray table with multiple Clorox wipes. The second thing I do is check the seat pocket for the "in case of motion discomfort" bag. Once we are airborne, the slightest jostle prompts me to commence humming "Silent Night" under my breath, an odd but surprisingly effective coping mechanism. I was convinced I would not survive twelve hours of air travel.

I survived. Barely. There was a lot of humming, and, despite the fact that the man next to me donned an eye mask, pushed in earbuds, queued up the latest *Batman* movie, and proceeded to sleep more soundly than I have ever slept in my very own bed, I did not sleep. Not five minutes in twelve hours. Instead, I was the lunatic standing in the back of the airplane next to the restrooms doing calisthenics while humming "Silent Night." What can I say? In addition to germ phobia and an inclination toward motion sickness, I also suffer from the occasional, inopportunely timed bout of restless leg syndrome.

Obviously, by the time I found myself sitting on the cool steps outside a Florence church with the rest of my group on my first day in Italy, I was bleary with exhaustion. I and the thirteen other participants in the Tuscany Writers' Retreat had gathered for a session with the spiritual director who would be with us on the trip. I don't remember much of what Jamin said to us that first night; my memories of the entire two days we spent in Florence are blurred by the effects of jet lag and sleep deprivation. In fact, I was so tired, when Jamin led us in prayer that evening outside the church, I bowed my head, closed my eyes, and pitched forward, asleep, off the step on which I was perched. Jolting awake mere seconds before dashing my face against the concrete, I glanced around to see if any of my fellow travelers had noticed my precarious slumber.

The one thing I do recall from that foggy first meeting is Jamin's advice that we each, to the best of our ability, release whatever expectations we had packed along with our Bibles, journals, and comfortable walking shoes. "God can and will work powerfully in you during this time," he assured us. "The Spirit may surprise you with something unexpected, *if* you allow yourself to be open to receive."

The next morning, Jamin sent us into the courtyard garden of our hotel for forty-five minutes of prayerful reflection and journaling. The theme of that morning's session was watchfulness. "Let not your thoughts float like feathers on the surface of the water, but sink to the bottom like lead," he advised before dismissing us.

I tucked myself into a wrought-iron chair in the shade of a towering hedge, opened my journal, and read the Scripture reading from the first chapter of Ephesians before moving on to the prompts: "Consider the ways in which you have seen God active and working in your life these past three months. To what degree have you been watchful of the story God has been writing in your life? Also consider the ways you have not been watchful of God's presence in your life. Ask God to show you the ways in which he has been present and active, but you have not been attending to such realities."

Immediately I began to record my response.

> How can I know where I'm going or what I should do if I don't know who I am? And how do I know who I am if I don't know who God is? The reason I'm not clear on what to do (my calling) is because I don't truly know who I am—my authentic self—and the reason I don't know who I am is because I don't truly know God in a deep and intimate way. In fact, I don't know if I know God at all. I don't know "the hope he has called me to" [Eph. 1:18] because I don't know him.

Paging through my journal a year later, I'm still shocked at the bald truth of the words I wrote that morning in the quiet courtyard. Yet I'm not altogether surprised that those were the thoughts that immediately bubbled to the surface on my very first day in Italy. Sheer exhaustion had opened me to a raw, vulnerable place. I was like the bare, exposed spot on the pin oak in my backyard. Stripped of my many layers of self-protection, in the hush of a Florentine courtyard, with no responsibilities to distract me and fatigue wearing me thin, a glimpse of my innermost self was visible for the first time in a long time. Perhaps for the first time ever.

The words I wrote in my journal that morning in response to the prompts and verses from Ephesians didn't surprise me in the moment, not because they weren't utterly unexpected—they were—but because I processed them through a haze of sleep deprivation. Jet lag stripped me of my defenses, but at the same time it protected me, wrapping my mind in fuzziness. Everything from those first two days—from what I ate and who I talked to, to what I saw and thought—was experienced as if through a layer of protective gauze. That morning in the courtyard I furiously scribbled my thoughts into my journal, and then, clapping the book shut with a thwap that echoed off the stone walls around me, I stood and joined my group for a tour of Florence. I didn't give the words I'd written another thought until the next day, when, well rested and refreshed, I was alone again.

It was Sunday morning, the Sabbath. Early the evening before, we'd arrived at the stunningly beautiful Villa La Foce in the heart of Tuscany. Following an alfresco breakfast under the wisteria-draped pergola and a spiritual session on the theme of rest, Jamin had dismissed us into the garden, journals in hand, to reflect and write.

"What does it mean for you that rest is found in God?" he'd asked us. "What does it mean that we are restless when we are away from him?"

I wandered La Foce's extensive grounds, noting the quiet spaces—a concrete bench and table tucked under an enormous, sculpted shrub; a shady patch of lush grass next to a row of fragrant lavender plants, bees burrowing into the blooms, the heady scent perfuming the morning air. The stone pavers tipped and clinked beneath my feet as I meandered, gliding my palm flat along the perfectly manicured hedge that ran parallel to the path. I stopped to take in the view— golden wheat fields, stately cypress lining a winding road, a haze settling low between the distant hills—and sighed with contentment, hardly able to believe that I was in Tuscany with an entire day of rest and enjoyment unfurling ahead of me.

I finally settled on a grassy spot beneath a grove of trees. Taking off my sandals, I sat with my back against a tree trunk, turned my face toward the Tuscan hills, and opened my journal. Except for the occasional buzzing of a nearby bee and the breeze in the leaves above my head, there was no noise—no traffic sounds, no human voices, no barking dogs, no tumble of a dryer or swish of a dishwasher. There was no agenda, no to-do list, no deadlines. It was just me, the view, and my own thoughts.

I wrote only one sentence in my journal during the forty-five minutes I spent under the Tuscan trees that morning: "I don't have rest in my life because I don't have rest in God." And with that single sentence, everything became devastatingly, heartbreakingly clear. Suddenly I knew why, months prior, the unnerving question about intimacy had floated to the surface during my daily quiet time on the park bench. Suddenly I knew the truth. I didn't have rest in my life because I didn't have rest in God. I didn't have clarity in my vocation, in my calling as a writer, because I didn't know who I was in God. I didn't know who I was, period, because I didn't know who I was *in God*. And I didn't know who I was in God because I didn't know God himself. In an instant I knew in my heart, mind, and marrow that every-thing, *everything*, begins with our relationship with God. And in an instant my heart broke, because I knew the truth: I didn't know God.

I cried underneath the Tuscan trees for forty-five minutes straight—not gentle, soft weeping, mind you, but nose-running, gulping, gasping sobbing. I didn't even have a sin-gle Kleenex with me—why would I have? I certainly hadn't wandered into one of the most beautiful, serene places on Earth expecting to have a complete and utter breakdown. I sweated. My hands shook. I was short of breath. My mouth went cottony, and I thought I might throw up, right there on the Tuscan hillside. Even when it was time to reconvene as a group beneath the pergola, I was barely able to keep my composure. I slid my sweaty feet out of my sandals and rested them on the stone pavers, grateful for the coolness on my soles as I swiped away the tears rolling from beneath my sunglasses.

I thought I'd come to Tuscany to find answers to my vocational unrest and to refill my creative and spiritual wells. But the truth revealed to me that morning was that I'd come to Tuscany to recognize, confront, and name my deepest brokenness. The truth was, I didn't know God. I didn't have a relationship with him. I still wrestled with deep questions of doubt and even, at times, with unbelief, and I still struggled fiercely in my faith.

## Stepping Out of Hiding

In the Gospel of Luke we are introduced to a woman who has suffered from incessant bleeding for twelve years. Desperate for a cure, Luke tells us, she slips in between the throngs of people who have gathered for a glimpse of the one proclaimed to be the Messiah. She creeps up behind Jesus and discreetly touches the hem of his robe, hoping beyond all reasonable hope that she will finally be healed. Jesus, feeling his power released, spins around, demanding to know who touched him. "When the woman realized that she couldn't remain hidden," Luke tells us, "she knelt trembling before him. In front of all the people, she blurted out her story—why she touched him and how at that same moment she was healed" (Luke 8:47 Message).

Read that bit again: *"When the woman realized that she couldn't remain hidden . . . she blurted out her story."* Why does the bleeding woman try to hide? Why does she want to remain hidden, invisible, unseen? Because she is ashamed of her condition, her brokenness. Rejected by society, she feels unworthy of love.

Like the bleeding woman, we, too, hide our worst selves, our shadow sides, from God. It's a little bit silly if you think about it—after all, God is omniscient and therefore knows our thoughts before we even think them ourselves. But it's true: we hide our most broken parts from God because we feel ashamed and unworthy of love.

Think for a moment about Adam and Eve in the Garden of Eden. After they succumb to temptation and eat the fruit from the Tree of the Knowledge of Good and Evil, what do the first man and woman, God's Beloved, do? They clothe themselves to hide their shame, and then, when they hear God strolling around the garden in the coolness of the evening, Adam and Eve hide from God himself (see Gen. 3:8). When God calls out, "Where are you?" (v. 9 Message), Adam answers, "I heard you in the garden and I was afraid because I was naked. And I hid" (v. 10 Message).

Adam does what we often do: he hides. Adam hides behind literal leaves and branches. He and Eve cover their naked bodies with fig leaves, and they hide amid the shadows of the trees. Adam also doesn't tell God the whole truth, at least at first. Instead, he stalls, saying only that he is afraid because he is naked. It's only when God demands a full confession from them that Adam and Eve ultimately name their sin (though even then, they don't take full responsibility: Adam blames Eve, and Eve blames the serpent).

Like Adam and Eve, we are ashamed and afraid, and so we hide too. We don't have fig leaves or the lush foliage of the Garden of Eden to shield ourselves, but we use our many figurative leaves and branches to camouflage ourselves just the same. And why? Because, like Adam and Eve, we don't trust God's goodness. We don't trust that he loves us enough to accept our whole flawed and broken selves. We don't fully believe he has our best interests in mind. And so we hedge our bets. We reveal only parts of our story, bits and pieces of our true selves, keeping our worst fears and our deepest sins hidden, not only from ourselves but from the One who knows us best.

> Fear and distrust prevent us from answering God's invitation into intimacy and healing.

Fear and distrust prevent us from answering God's invitation into intimacy and healing. Fear and distrust prevent us from standing, picking up our mats, and walking. Like the bleeding woman and Adam and Eve in the garden, we often only step out of hiding to tell our story when we are called out by God himself.

## Answering God's Call to Name Your Deepest Brokenness

As I mentioned earlier, I am a type Three in the Enneagram personality type system. Often called "The Achiever" or, perhaps even more telling, "The Performer," Threes are "ambitious, competent, and energetic, status-conscious and highly driven for advancement. They are diplomatic and poised, but can also be overly concerned with their image and what others think of them." Threes also typically have problems with workaholism and competitiveness, and our key motivations are affirmation, attention, admiration, and to be distinguished from others. In short, we Threes aspire to present our best selves at all times. Failure is anathema to Threes, and therefore we avoid it at all costs, even at the expense of authenticity and, at times, truth.[1]

Each Enneagram type is associated with a particular sin, and for Threes, the sin is deceit. When I first learned I was a Three, I was initially surprised by the fact that my hallmark sin is deceit. It didn't make sense to me that a writer, particularly a writer who has written a memoir, would be deceitful. After all, I reasoned, isn't memoir the be-all-and-end-all of truth-telling and authenticity? Aren't memoir writers the *most* transparent, the *most* authentic?

I realize now that "transparent" memoir writing was actually a way for me to control my story and the image of myself that I presented to others and to my own self. I didn't fabricate any parts of my story, but I see now how I used humor in my memoir as a way to convince people to like me, as well as a shield to protect myself from the judgment of others, and perhaps even to protect myself from hard truths about myself.

Turns out, I've been using humor this way for a long time. My sister and I actually have a name for it: we call it "clowning out." She does it too. When we find ourselves in a potentially awkward or uncomfortable social situation, or among people we want to impress, we perform. The hallmarks of clowning out include highly animated storytelling, often with ourselves as the butt of the joke; wild gesticulating; loud, fast talking; maniacal laughter; and general buffoonery. Our intent is to entertain people, make them laugh, and ultimately, make them like us. Not only is clowning out exhausting—sometimes I feel like a circus monkey, performing tricks for approval and dancing as fast as I can—it's also a remarkably effective way of keeping others at arm's length. If I'm the performer, I control the show. And in controlling the show, I can choose how much or how little I want to reveal of myself and how close I will allow myself to get to someone else. Clowning out, and, to some extent, my use of humor overall, are yet more leaves on my tree—manifestations of my false self that's clamoring to create a sense of worth and identity.

Your deepest brokenness is likely not the same as mine. Your tree contains a different variety of branches and leaves. My shadow side is doubt, and for most of my life, I've used busyness, productivity, striving, achievement, and even humor as masks to shield myself from this deepest, darkest part of myself. I don't know what your shadow side is, but I do know this: you have one. We all do. There is undoubtedly something that, unless it's acknowledged, will inhibit you from entering into intimate relationship with God. Maybe it's lack of trust or need for control. Maybe the deep wounds you carry from your past are a barrier between you and God. Maybe it's something else entirely. Only you can identify your false self. Only you can answer God's call to name your deepest brokenness, and only you can offer that brokenness up to God.

> Only you can identify your false self. Only you can answer God's call to name your deepest brokenness, and only you can offer that brokenness up to God.

## Fearing Our Deepest Desires

"We are not good at recognizing illusions," Thomas Merton wrote, "least of all the ones we have about ourselves—the ones we are born with and which feed the roots of sin."[2] I am a master at deception, and there is no one I have deceived more than myself. I refused to face my deepest flaws and my darkest sins because I was afraid they were unforgiveable and made me unredeemable and unlovable. Like Adam and Eve, I hid among the trees. The dense foliage of my life—busyness, distraction, social media, my to-do list, and, above all, my striving to achieve, succeed, and please—protected me from my deepest self, from both my sins and my desires. Like the bleeding woman, I told my story—I confessed—only when I was called out and could stay hidden no more.

As Ruth Haley Barton observes, "It can be frightening to allow ourselves to want something we're not sure we can have, especially if it is something as essential as the presence of God in our lives. In many of us, the fear of not getting what our heart longs for has led us to develop an unconscious pattern of distancing ourselves from our desire in order to avoid the pain of its lack of fulfillment."[3] I couldn't bring myself to face the fact that even after my return to faith, even after writing a whole book about that journey back to God, even after pursuing a career and calling as a Christian writer, I *still* wrestled with doubt and unbelief. I couldn't name it, not only because acknowledging my struggle made me feel like a complete and utter fraud, but also because while my deepest desire was to know God, my deepest fear was that to know him was, for me, impossible.

I didn't realize it that morning, but my revelation under the Tuscan trees was a confession of sorts. Like Jesus, who called out the bleeding woman who had touched his robe, God called me out and demanded I tell my story—the whole story. For the first time in a long time I admitted both to myself and to God that I still wrestled with unbelief. I revealed my sin, my shadow side. I named my deepest brokenness, and in doing so, gave voice not only to my sin, but also to my desire.

Remember the words I quoted from Ruth Haley Barton in chapter 2? "The willingness to see ourselves as we are and name it in God's presence is at the very heart of the spiritual journey."[4] In that moment on the ground in Tuscany, I saw myself as I was, and I named it in God's presence. Like the bleeding woman who only confessed when she realized she could not remain hidden, I knew, in that moment, that I could no longer stay hidden, that I had, in fact, never been hidden. I saw my sin—that I didn't know God—and my desire—that I yearned to know God.

For the first time in my life I saw and understood that relationship with God is the foundation of everything. I saw that all things—intimacy in marriage, parenting, and friendships; relationship to community; vocation; knowledge of self—are built on knowing and being in relationship with God. I saw that my identity as a child of God is everything. I saw that without that, I have nothing; without that, I am nothing. I finally named not only my brokenness but my desire to be whole. Like the man by the pool of Bethesda, I finally heard and answered Jesus' question. I answered, *Yes, I want to get well*, and I picked up my mat.

Is there some piece of yourself or your story that is inhibiting you from understanding and stepping into your true identity as a beloved child of God? It may not be doubt or unbelief keeping you from experiencing the fullness of God's presence, like it was (and sometimes, if I am totally honest, still is) for me. It may be something different altogether—perhaps a past wound, a deep fear, a lack of trust, or a need for control. God is calling you like he called Adam and Eve, like he called the hemorrhaging woman, to step out of hiding—to recognize and confront yourself as you really are and name it in God's presence. God is calling you to stand, pick up your mat, and walk like the man at the pool of Bethesda toward him.

I need to tell you, though, that this stepping out, this walking toward, won't necessarily be easy. In fact, the way it played out for me that morning under the Tuscan trees and in the aftermath of my revelation was not beautiful at all. It was not a peaceful, joyful epiphany with singing cherubs and a crescendo of violins. It was not a moment of healing, hope, and freedom like it was for the bleeding woman who touched the hem of Jesus' robe or the invalid at the pool of Bethesda who rose triumphantly to his feet.

My moment of confession, of stepping out of hiding and into the blinding light of truth, was the opposite. It was terrifying and painful, dark, lonely, and empty. It felt wildly out of control, a visceral experience not unlike a labor of sorts. I didn't understand what was happening. I thought I was having a panic attack. I wondered if I'd simply drunk too much strong Italian coffee that morning at breakfast; I thought maybe the mix of jet lag and caffeine had produced a cataclysmic chemical reaction in my body.

91

In fact, it wasn't the effects of caffeine or jet lag or even a panic attack. Naming my sin and my desire, as painful and frightening as that was, was my first tenuous but necessary step toward uncovering my true self, but it was also a step into uncertainty. What I experienced on the Tuscan hillside that morning was, I know now, a plunge into the dark night of the soul.

## GOING DEEPER

It's no coincidence that my revelation took place on that Tuscan hillside, but it was the uninterrupted solitude and the quiet rather than the setting itself that made the difference. Freed from the constraints of my daily five minutes, I had plenty of opportunity in which to settle deep into my thoughts, and when I did, the parts of myself that I'd avoided for so long quickly made themselves known.

Stepping out of hiding, acknowledging your false self, and naming your deepest brokenness is daunting work, but I urge you to continue to take time, as you are able, to sit quietly in solitude and allow this process to unfold and take shape. Here are some questions to consider as you begin to recognize and name both your sins and your deepest desires:

1. Do you ever feel that God is calling you out of hiding? What parts of your story could you be keeping from yourself and from God? Where are you most comfortable hiding? What might that tell you in terms of identifying your true self?

2. Consider the questions Jamin asked my retreat group: "What does it mean for you that rest is found in God? What does it mean that we are restless when we are away from him?" Do those questions provoke any thoughts or stir any emotions in you? Do you feel restful or restless these days?

3. Why do you think God called out "Where are you?" to Adam and Eve when they were hiding in the garden?

4. What illusions do you have about yourself? How can they "feed the roots of [your] sin," as Thomas Merton said? Why do you think you hold on to them?

5. Are you ready to name your sins?

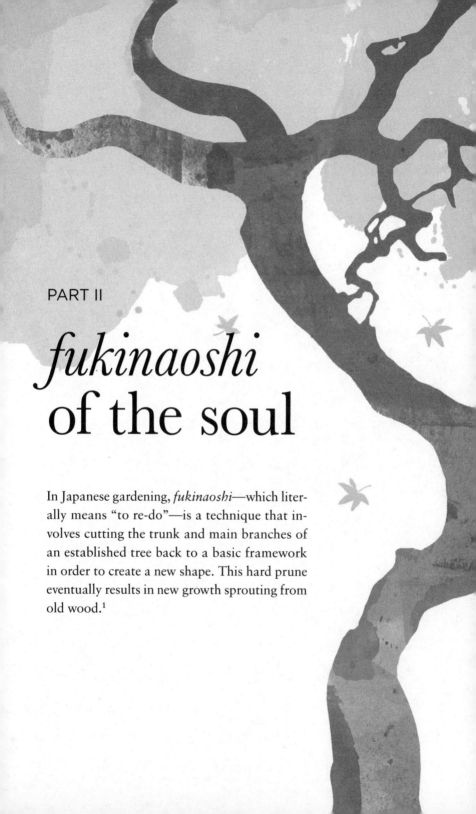

PART II

# *fukinaoshi* of the soul

In Japanese gardening, *fukinaoshi*—which literally means "to re-do"—is a technique that involves cutting the trunk and main branches of an established tree back to a basic framework in order to create a new shape. This hard prune eventually results in new growth sprouting from old wood.[1]

# 5

# the hard prune

## Letting go of the last handhold

The maiming became the sculpting. The paring
back gave way to a vigorous flourishing.

—Mark Buchanan, *Spiritual Rhythms: Being
with Jesus Every Season of Your Soul*

With the publication of some of her private letters in 2007, ten years after her death, many around the world were shocked to discover that Mother Teresa had struggled for decades with a crisis of faith. The letters she wrote to her confessor are surprising, unnerving even, especially in light of her lifelong, faithful work as a Catholic nun committed to serving the poor and destitute in Calcutta. While Mother Teresa was living, only two or three of her very closest confidantes were aware of her intense personal suffering and struggle. The rest of the world witnessed only her smiling face, her humble demeanor, and her selfless acts of service.

"Pray for me—for within me everything is icy cold.—It is only that blind faith that carries me through for in reality to me all is darkness," she wrote to her archbishop in 1955.[1] "Darkness is such that I really do not see—neither with my mind nor my reason.—The place of God in my soul is blank.—There is no God in me . . . He does not want me—He is not there . . . Sometimes—I just hear my own heart cry out—'My God' and nothing else comes.—The torture and pain I can't explain," she wrote six years later to her friend Father Joseph Neuner.[2] Unbeknownst to the world until long after her death, Mother Teresa suffered from a long and relentless dark night of the soul.

The dark night of the soul takes its name from a sixteenth-century poem written by Spanish Carmelite friar Juan De Yepes Y Alvarez. Known as Juan de la Cruz, or John of the Cross, Alvarez founded the first monastery for the radical Discalced (derived from the Latin word meaning "barefoot") Carmelites in Spain in 1568. When the traditional Carmelites outlawed the renegade Discalced sect, they imprisoned Alvarez, and it was during his nine months in jail that he wrote his nine-stanza poem—titled simply *Noche Oscura*—*Dark Night*—as well as the accompanying line-by-line exposition. Together the poem and explication have come to be known as *The Dark Night of the Soul*.

St. John of the Cross understood the dark night of the soul to be a necessary part of the spiritual journey toward greater wholeness and intimacy with God. He saw this period of darkness and estrangement from God as a purification process, a painful but necessary purgation, or stripping away, that ultimately leads to clarity, or what he called illumination. "God leads into the dark night those whom He desires to purify from all these imperfections so that He may bring them farther onward," St. John of the Cross explained. "God grants the soul in this state the favor of purging it and healing it with this strong lye of bitter purgation. . . . In this way God makes it to die to all that is not naturally God, so that, once it is stripped and denuded of its former skin, He may begin to clothe it anew."³ St. John of the Cross understood the dark night of the soul to be a painful but ultimately good and fruitful experience.

Don't be fooled by St. John's language, though. This "favor of purging," as he so delicately put it, is not typically a pleasant process. Coming face-to-face with your baggage— your sins, your wounds and pain, and the behavioral patterns you've created as a defense against these wounds and pain—is difficult. Likewise, beginning the process of allowing God to strip all that away can be terrifying, isolating, and very painful. This is the moment in Psalm 69 when David cries out:

> Save me, O God,
>     for the waters have come up to my neck.
> I sink in the miry depths,
>     where there is no foothold.
> I have come into the deep waters;
>     the floods engulf me.
> I am worn out calling for help;
>     my throat is parched.
> My eyes fail,
>     looking for my God. (vv. 1–3)

In the process of stripping away and dying to self, there is often an accompanying feeling of hopelessness and the sense of abandonment by God. In this moment, up to your neck in "the miry depths," grappling for a foothold, something, anything, to stand on, our first inclination is often to deny or resist such a painful process. This resistance can be overt—we might outright refuse to acknowledge God's prodding, like I did the day I heard the question about intimacy while I sat in silence on the park bench. Or it can be subtle—we may use the busyness of our lives to distract us from God's invitation into purgation.

The morning in the garden in Tuscany, when I suddenly saw so clearly the ways in which I'd been hiding from God, my first instinct was "fight or flight." Part of me wanted to deny the revelation, to squash what was becoming known to me down into my deepest recesses and back from wherever it had come, to let the branches and leaves that had shielded me for so long swing back into place. The other part of me simply wanted to flee, to dash down the cypress-lined road and up and over the distant hillside, to run myself into physical exhaustion and away from the spiritual and emotional upheaval that was ravaging my body and soul.

My resistance that morning was strong and obvious, but looking back, I see now that I'd been resisting this descent into the dark night of the soul for a long time in much more subtle ways—by distracting myself with my to-do list, by being "insanely busy," by filling my spare moments with social media, and by not making room for silence and stillness in my life.

The irony, of course, was that morning in Tuscany I could neither fight nor flee the invitation into purgation. There was nowhere for me to go. I had no to-do list or errands or work deadlines to draw my attention away from the frightening revelation at hand. I was alone with an abundance of solitude in a foreign country, six long days from my flight home. I simply had too much time on my hands to escape from my own thoughts and the desires of my soul. There was no other choice but to freefall into the abyss that yawned before me. That morning in Tuscany I was finally forced to "let go of the very last handhold," as Barton says, "the handhold of the self we have created in response to the wounds of our life in an imperfect world."[4] That day under the trees in the garden, I tumbled hard, tearing limbs and branches as I went.

## *Fukinaoshi* of the Soul

*Fukinaoshi* is a hard prune, usually done during the autumn or winter, when a tree is resting in its dormant phase and thus less likely to resist with various defenses or succumb to infection or disease as a result of the cutting. The gardener makes a number of dramatic cuts, removing whole limbs and branches in order to reduce the tree to its most basic framework. The aim of *fukinaoshi*, says Japanese aesthetic gardener Jake Hobson, is to prune unwanted branches both to reveal the essential shape of the trunk and make it easier to work on the remaining branches in the future. Work slowly but confidently, advises Hobson, and "understand right from the start that this sort of pruning will not harm the tree."[5]

Entry into the dark night is the *fukinaoshi* of the soul, when God, the Master Gardener, makes the first deep, dramatic cuts necessary on the journey toward uncovering our

101

truest, most authentic self. As Jake Hobson observes, to the untrained eye, *fukinaoshi* can look rather extreme. He describes it as the transition from a tree to a carcass and then, ultimately, back to a tree again—albeit a tree that looks markedly different from the original. The process can also look and, at least from the tree's perspective, feel harmful and dangerous, but when done correctly, it's not.

*Fukinaoshi* of the soul is much the same. Stripped of our false selves—the array of extraneous leaves and branches we have long used as a camouflaging shield—we stand naked and vulnerable before God and our own selves. As with the pruning of a tree, our own pruning can look and even feel harmful. Pruning hurts; it wounds us and then leaves scars. But remember what Hobson said: this sort of pruning will not harm the tree, and likewise, it will not ultimately harm us, as painful as the actual process feels.

In *fukinaoshi* of the soul we are like the remaining carcass of a pruned tree: bare, exposed, and, at least to the untrained eye—particularly our own—dead. Except we are not dead; we have merely lost our life in order for it to be saved (see Luke 9:23–24). Like the dramatically pruned tree, which is in a dormant state but still very much alive, the core of our true self is alive and well. Our deepest, truest, most essential self has been waiting all along for this opportunity to be uncovered and exposed to the light, waiting for the invitation to grow into its fullest, richest, most beautiful potential.

> Our deepest, truest, most essential self has been waiting all along for this opportunity to be uncovered and exposed to the light, waiting for the invitation to grow into its fullest, richest, most beautiful potential.

## Mystery and Paradox

There is deep contradiction and paradox here, and if you're anything like me, your brain is pushing hard against this concept of cutting back in order to reveal and thrive, dying in order to flourish. For instance, you may be wondering how my admission of deep doubt could have possibly been beneficial in any way. How could naming my deepest, most secret sin—unbelief—possibly pave the way toward a truer relationship and deeper intimacy with God? You're probably thinking that doesn't make one bit of sense.

I hear you. It doesn't make sense. That was my exact reaction when I first read Mother Teresa's heartbreaking confessions of her own darkness and unbelief. My brain couldn't wrap itself around the fact that she confessed and prayed about her unbelief *to Jesus himself.* At the urging of her confessor, Mother Teresa addressed one of her most intimate letters to Christ. "In my soul I feel just that terrible pain of loss—of God not wanting me—of God not being God—of God not really existing (Jesus, please forgive my blasphemies—I have been told to write everything)," she wrote. "If there be no God—there can be no soul.—If there is no soul then Jesus—You also are not true. . . . I am afraid to write all those terrible things that pass in my soul.—They must hurt you."[6]

*Wait, what?* I thought when I first read those words. *How does one confess unbelief while at the same time addressing that statement of unbelief to the one in whom one doesn't believe?* It didn't make sense.

And yet it does. Reading Mother Teresa's letters now, several years after I first encountered them, I understand how that tension between belief and unbelief can exist. I understand that Mother Teresa's faith transcended either/ or, yes/no, black/white. In naming her pain—even the pain of darkness and unbelief—she was, paradoxically, drawing closer to God, even when she herself couldn't perceive God's presence. Richard Rohr explains the paradox like this:

> Many mystics speak of the God-experience as simultaneously falling into an abyss and being grounded. This sounds like a contradiction, but in fact, when you allow yourself to fall into the abyss . . . you discover it's somehow a rich, supportive, embracing spaciousness where you don't have to ask (or answer) the questions of whether you're right or wrong. You're being held and so you do not need to try to "hold" yourself together.[7]

When we acknowledge our deepest brokenness, we acknowledge our fullest, deepest selves—our whole selves. And it is only when we present that self—stripped naked, 100 percent whole and true—that we are truly able to meet God and allow ourselves to be held by his love. God doesn't want just the best parts of our selves—the parts we've polished and prettied up with a fancy silk bow. He desires the worst parts of our selves most of all—the parts we despise, the parts we are afraid of, the parts we most want to hide from the world, from our own selves, and from him. He even wants the part of us that doesn't have faith or trust in him.

"God meets us where we are, not where we pretend to be or wish we were," says psychologist Dr. Larry Crabb. "God's truth does not set free a pretending or hiding heart."[8] I pretended to be and wished with all my heart that I was an upstanding Christian, my faith rock solid, my belief in God steadfast. That's who I wanted to present to others and to God, but it's not the whole truth of who I was (and often still am). Likewise, you may pretend to be or wish you were something or someone else—trusting, surrendered, forgiving, confident, grounded, at peace—but the truth is, God won't meet you there, because he is not interested in meeting your false, pretending self. He wants YOU—flaws, sins, brokenness, and all.

God is in the deepest recesses of your soul, in your most broken places, in the parts of yourself you most want to hide. "The soul is healed by confession. Sin splits the self," says John Ortberg. "As long as I keep pretending, my soul keeps dying."[9] In short, God is often where you least expect to find him. God comes to you and loves you where you are, not where you think you should be. Once you understand this truth, you will, as Dr. Crabb says, be set free.

This was the beautiful irony, paradox, and radical grace of my confession on the Tuscan hillside. The admission of both my deepest brokenness (my continuing struggle with doubt and unbelief) and my deepest desire (to know God, to love him, and to know my belovedness in him) set my true self free. As I said earlier, it wasn't an angels-singing-cherubs-frolicking kind of revelation. It didn't happen instantaneously (and we'll get to the waiting aspects of this journey in chapter 7). But it was the beginning.

Letting go and allowing ourselves to fall headlong into the dark abyss is the beginning of our grounding in God. In short, we have to fall before we land. This is, as Rohr says, "the ultimate paradox of the God experience: 'falling into the hands of the living God' (Heb. 10:31)." This experience isn't something we understand rationally, but rather, something we know intuitively, at the soul level. "When you can lend yourself to it and not fight it or explain it, falling into the abyss is ironically an experience of ground, of the rock, of the foundation," Rohr explains. "This is totally counterintuitive. Your dualistic, logical mind can't get you there. It can only be known experientially. That's why the mystics use magnificent metaphors—none of them adequate or perfect—for this experience. 'It's like . . . It's like . . . ,' they love to say."[10]

I'll say it metaphorically too. It's like you are a tree, standing in the middle of a garden, your elegant, stately shape obscured by a tangle of leaves and branches. A gardener comes along, tools in hand, and you let him slowly begin to remove the mess, limb by limb, branch by branch, leaf by leaf. It's painful, this removal of your covering. It's taken a long time to grow the many layers of this elaborate shield; so long, in fact, that you cannot remember what it's like to live without it. As bits and pieces of your innermost self are revealed, you feel exposed and afraid.

> Letting go and allowing ourselves to fall headlong into the dark abyss is the beginning of our grounding in God. In short, we have to fall before we land.

Finally, the gardener is finished. You stand alone in the middle of the garden, your naked trunk open to the elements. You feel ugly, diminished, vulnerable, and broken. You do not recognize this new you. You cannot yet see the beauty and goodness that is there. You cannot yet feel that your roots are firmly planted in fertile ground.

That's how I felt on the Tuscan hillside and in the weeks and months I walked through my own dark night of the soul.

I was shaken—devastated by my lack of faith, by the unbelief I'd hidden from for so long, now revealed in the light of day. I felt raw and vulnerable. I did not recognize myself. I could not see, as I would later, that the fall is an inextricable part of the rising.

## Sometimes We Have to Be Forcibly Turned

My second-born was breech in the womb—head up, feet down. I knew something wasn't quite right even before the obstetrician confirmed it at my thirty-six-week appointment. My body told me . . . or rather, the baby did. His head, lodged just under my sternum, caused significant shortness of breath, and his tiny feet jabbed almost nonstop at my bladder and pelvis. I could feel that he was positioned the wrong way.

When an ultrasound revealed the baby was breech, my doctor laid out two choices. We could schedule a cesarean section. Or we could try a procedure called external cephalic version—ECV or "version" for short—in which she would attempt to turn the baby manually. Version is only about 50 percent successful, but, surgery-phobe that I am, a 50/50 shot at success was enough for me. We scheduled the inpatient procedure to take place at the local hospital later that week.

I'd learned enough about ECV to know it wasn't going to be an easy-breezy walk in the park, so in the days leading up to the procedure, I tried every old-wives'-tale trick in the book to prompt the baby to turn on his own. I propped one end of a closed ironing board on the edge of the sofa and lay on it, my head pitched toward the floor, feet in the air, hoping gravity would work its magic. I attempted, with great awkwardness and much failure, to stand the entire weight of my giantess pregnant body on my head. I did squats and jumping jacks and lunges and waddled mile after mile up and down my street and around and around my block. All to no avail; the baby refused to turn.

The version was performed by two doctors who stood on either side of me, each with her hands on the surface of my enlarged abdomen, one set of hands by the baby's head and the other by his bottom. I was hooked to a fetal heart monitor and injected with a medication to relax my uterus and help prevent contractions. "Remember, if it's too much, you can tell us to stop at any time," my obstetrician reminded me right before beginning the procedure—not exactly a confidence or courage booster. On the count of three, the two doctors simultaneously pressed hard on my stomach, manipulating the baby's position inside the uterus from head-up to head-down. Meanwhile, though I'd been instructed to do the "eeee," "ooooh," and "ahhhh" of Lamaze, all I could manage was to squinch my eyes shut, grit my teeth, and hold my breath.

For the record, a version feels as medieval as it sounds. Though he was less than seven pounds, the baby's forced roll inside my uterus felt like a tsunami rippling through my torso. My husband, who observed the procedure over one of the doctor's shoulders, described it as "a scene out of *Alien*" (thankfully he mentioned this later, rather than during the process). Although it felt much longer, it was all over in a matter of seconds, and the version was successful. The baby was forcibly turned, and he stayed in the proper head-down position until his birth a few weeks later.

The version is a fitting metaphor for the process of spiritual rebirth and transformation. In other words, we don't always surrender peacefully and amicably to God's invitation to change our ways. Sometimes, especially if you're inclined to stiff-necked-ness like me, you have to be forcibly turned. Like my son in the womb, we are often stubborn. We like circumstances to stay exactly the same, thank you very much. Sometimes, because we are not willing or able to turn ourselves, we need God to turn us, and in that turn, there is discomfort. "Whenever we say no to one way of life that we have long been used to, there is pain," Eugene Peterson acknowledges. When there is a "decisive intervention . . . the procedure hurts, but the results are healthy."[11]

Rowan's heart rate plummeted for a few seconds immediately after he was manually turned in utero by my obstetrician and her colleague. This was expected; a version can be stressful for a fetus. Turning Rowan in utero was a decisive intervention; the procedure hurt, but the results were necessary, healthy, and good. Likewise, an experience of the dark night of the soul, in which we turn (or are forcibly turned) to face our shadow side, are stripped of our defensive armor, and turn back to stand naked before God, is an intervention, a decisive dismantling of our status quo that is often painful but ultimately necessary, healthy, and good.

This is exactly what Paul experienced on his journey to Damascus (see Acts 9). A notorious persecutor of the early disciples of Jesus, Paul (who was known as Saul at the time) was traveling from Jerusalem to Damascus with arrest warrants for "any there who belonged to the Way" (Acts 9:2), when he was suddenly dazzled by a brilliant flash of light.

As he crumpled to the ground, a voice boomed from above, "Saul, Saul, why do you persecute me?" (v. 4). Discovering he had lost all sight in the mysterious exchange, Saul stood and was led by his companions to Damascus, where he languished blind, hungry, and thirsty for three days until Ananias, obeying God's command, restored Saul's sight and proclaimed him to be filled with the Holy Spirit. Brimming with clarity, faith, and a new mission, Paul went on to become a founder of the early Christian church and one of the greatest evangelists of all time.

Most of us are so familiar with Paul's tremendous contributions to Christianity, we forget that before he became St. Paul he had to be forcibly and painfully turned by God toward God. That frightening experience on the road to Damascus and the three harrowing days of darkness, hunger, and thirst that followed was Paul's literal and figurative dark night of the soul.

The Bible doesn't tell us what those three days of blindness and fasting in Damascus were like for Paul, but we can assume it was neither an easy nor a pleasant experience. In fact, we can assume those days were probably among the most difficult and painful in Paul's life—a rock-bottom period of self-reckoning in which Paul, alone in the darkness with ample time on his hands, was forced to turn toward his shadow side, face his deepest brokenness, and walk through it and out the other side.

Paul did not plan for or choose this intervention, and the subsequent dismantling of self that occurred was undoubtedly difficult and exceedingly painful. But the results of that turning and transformation changed Christianity and the world. Stripped of his false self, Paul emerged from darkness, stepped into the baptismal waters, and was reborn into the man God had created him to be.

## Your Name Will No Longer Be Jacob

Solitude, says Henri Nouwen, is "the place of conversion, the place where the old self dies and the new self is born. . . . The struggle is real because the danger is real. It is the danger of living the whole of our life as one long defense against the reality of our condition."[12] This is the key issue, and questions beg to be asked: What is the reality of your condition? What is it you are so vigorously defending against? What are your greatest fears and your deepest desires? Will you allow a *fukinaoshi* of your soul? Will you submit to the decisive intervention? Indeed, like Paul and, as we will see, like Jacob, you may have to be forcibly turned.

Many years after leaving home, Jacob, son of Isaac, decided to return to his homeland and his family with his two wives and his eleven sons (see Gen. 31–33). The Genesis story tells us that Jacob hadn't left home on good terms. He had betrayed his father and deceived his brother, and as a result he had hightailed it out of Canaan, fearing for his life. Jacob stayed away for a long time, and he knew he would have many amends to make upon his return.

When they reached the Jabbok River on their journey home, Jacob ensured his wives, sons, servants, and his many possessions made it safely across the water. Strangely, though, Jacob himself stayed on the other side of the river by himself and prepared to sleep alone on the riverbank that night. This detail has always struck me. I often wonder why Jacob didn't cross the river with his family. Was it simple cowardice? Was Jacob offering up his family and possessions, hoping to appease his angry brother so that Esau would decide not to hurt him? Or was there perhaps another, deeper reason he stayed on the other side? Could he have realized that he needed the time, stillness, and space of the dark night in which to work through the heavy emotional baggage he carried as he journeyed toward home?

Genesis tells us Jacob was approached during the night by a man (some translations refer to the man as an angel) who wrestled with him until daybreak. The two were apparently evenly matched, until the man, seeing that he could not overpower Jacob, touched Jacob's hip and injured him. Then the man said to Jacob, "Let me go, for it is daybreak" (Gen. 32:26).

This experience on the riverbank was Jacob's descent into the dark night of the soul, a literal and figurative wrestling with God in the darkness. Jacob had a lot to work through with God on that riverbank. Deceitful, manipulative, controlling, and power-hungry, his false self had dominated for years, but it was there, in the dark of night, that Jacob was reconciled both to God and to his true self. Like my son in the womb, Paul on the road to Damascus, and me on the Tuscan hillside, Jacob did not turn easily or willingly on his own. It was a painful battle, one that left him with a lasting limp.

I find the next part of this story particularly intriguing. Refusing to let go of the man, Jacob demanded a blessing from him. In response, the man asked Jacob a puzzling question, seemingly out of nowhere and appearing, at least initially, to have little to do with the encounter at hand. "What is your name?" the strange man asked Jacob (v. 27).

In Hebrew, the name Jacob is *Ya'aqob,* which is translated as "heel holder."[13] This makes sense when you consider that when he was born, Jacob emerged from the womb gripping his twin brother Esau's heel. A closer look at the root of *Ya'aqob,* however, reveals some interesting details that shed additional light on Jacob's name and character. For example, the root of *Ya'aqob* comes from the verb *'aqab,* which not only means "to take by the heel," but also to "supplant," "overreach," or "assail."[14] Likewise, the adjective *'aqob* means "deceitful," "sly," "insidious," or "slippery."[15]

All of this makes perfect sense in the context of Jacob's story as the second-born son who deceived his father, stole his brother's birthright and blessing, and fled before he could be made to pay for his transgressions. Jacob wasn't simply the twin who grabbed his brother's heel at birth. He was also the insidious, deceitful younger sibling who circumvented tradition and supplanted his brother as the rightful inheritor in order to gain the power and control he desired.

In demanding that Jacob state his name before he blessed him, God insisted that Jacob come face-to-face with his whole history, including his past, his faults, his mistakes, and his sins. In the moment Jacob stated his name before God, he stepped out of hiding. He was, for the first time ever, finally willing to see himself as he really was and, quite literally, name it in God's presence. This was his transformative moment, the moment in which he shed his false self and was made new by God.

"Your name will no longer be Jacob, but Israel," God proclaimed, "because you have struggled with God and with humans and have overcome" (Gen. 32:28). As the sun rose behind him and the dark night receded into morning, Jacob limped away from the place he'd met God face-to-face. God had intervened, there had been pain, but rebirthed and renamed, Jacob—Israel—was set free on the bank of the Jabbok River to live into the person God had created him to be.

Your dark night of the soul may not be as dramatic as Jacob's or Paul's or as long as Mother Teresa's, and it may not manifest itself physically in the same way it did for me. Nonetheless, you have a shadow side—some aspects of yourself that are not aligned with God's vision for you. Confronting your false self and naming it is a necessary and critical part of deep transformation. Though it doesn't feel like it in the moment, the dark night—the *fukinaoshi* of the soul—is the opening into a deeper, more authentic union with God. The loneliness, fear, and sense of abandonment you feel during the dark night is the result of the stripping and emptying, but it is also this stripping and emptying that creates the space for God to enter in. As Ruth Haley Barton says, "Emptiness is prerequisite to being filled. The presence of God is poured out most generously when there is space in our souls to receive him."[16]

The dark night of the soul is the pivot point, the most critical moment on the journey toward uncovering and discovering your true self. Will you accept God's invitation to let go of the last handhold? Will you allow yourself to be turned, or will you require a forcible intervention? Will you cling to your many branches and leaves, or will you cede to the Gardener's shears? Will you open yourself to the difficult but necessary *fukinaoshi* of the soul? The hard prune, allowing yourself to be cut back to your basic, most essential framework, opens the way for the first tender shoot to sprout from old wood.

## GOING DEEPER

Author and pastor Mark Buchanan describes the hard prune as a maiming that ultimately becomes a sculpting.[17] There is pain, a wounding, before there is healing and flourishing. Be gentle with yourself during this *fukinaoshi* of the soul. You are moving toward openness, exposure, and vulnerability, yet this is also a process that cannot be rushed. The questions bubbling to the surface may not be answered immediately, or perhaps ever. Now is the time, as the poet Rainer Maria Rilke advises, "to have patience with everything that remains unsolved in your heart."[18]

Here are some questions to consider as you begin to yield to the Master Gardener's shears:

1. Why do you think God leads into the dark night those he desires to purify, as St. John of the Cross said?

2. Have you ever walked through a painful but ultimately fruitful dark night in your life? What did you learn?

3. Is there a handhold you are being asked to let go of right now? How does the idea of letting go make you feel?

4. Consider, as Mother Teresa did, writing a letter to Jesus in which you name your deepest brokenness, the part of you that you have tried to hide. Is it possible for you to believe that God loves even this part of you?

5. If you could receive a new name from God, as Jacob did, what would it be? Why that particular name?

# 6

# the far side of the wilderness

Following God, even when
you can't see the way through

To learn something new, take the path today that
you took yesterday.

—John Burroughs, naturalist

I realize that in describing my descent into the dark night,
I'm not making a great case for the benefits of silence and
solitude. After all, who wants to succumb to sobbing and
sweating feet as the result of a little quiet time? But the truth
is, and I cannot stress this strongly enough, silence and solitude are an absolute necessity if we truly desire to know and
understand our true selves and enter into intimate relationship with God. It's nonnegotiable. You will not come to
know your whole self and who you are in God if you do not

make a concerted effort to carve out space for silence and solitude in the midst of your everyday life.

Please know that you don't need to travel to Tuscany to seek out quiet and contemplation. True, it was wonderful to have the opportunity and, frankly, the luxury to immerse myself in beauty and in copious amounts of silence and solitude for ten consecutive days, but it wasn't the place itself that provoked my hillside revelation. It was the uninterrupted quiet and space, time completely free of distraction and responsibility on the far side of the wilderness that opened the door to God's invitation.

You're probably familiar with the story of Moses and the burning bush. It's a Sunday school staple, and for good reason—God doesn't speak from a flaming shrub every day, after all. A couple of years ago, though, I noticed something in this story that I'd never seen before, a new-to-me detail I'd never considered, which is this: just prior to spotting the burning bush, Moses, the text tells us, was tending his flock of sheep at "the far side of the wilderness" (Exod. 3:1).

*The far side of the wilderness.* Those are the six words I'd never before noticed in a story I'd read or listened to a dozen or more times. Maybe in my eagerness to get to the heart of the story I'd always skimmed past the opening sentence. Or maybe I'd never really considered the implications of what being at the far side of the wilderness really means. The more I thought about it, though, the more I realized that these are some of the most important words in this story. Because here's the truth: God didn't just lead Moses into the wilderness; he led Moses to the *far side* of the wilderness—to the

118

quietest, loneliest, most isolated, most desolate place possible. And it was only in that place, away from the demands
and distractions of ordinary life, that God spoke to Moses.

What if that burning bush had been alongside a more
traveled path? Would Moses, immersed in the demands and
distractions of a typical day, have even noticed a shrub spark-
ing with flames? Would he have ambled over, curious, to take
a closer look? Would he have even stopped at all?

We'd like to think so. We'd like to think we, too, would notice something as highly unusual as a burning bush and would
stop to investigate such a puzzling and intriguing sight. But
let's recall how many commuters, intent on hustling to their
next task, barreled past one of the world's most renowned
classical musicians performing "Ave Maria" on his Stradivarius violin in the middle of an urban metro station. A rare and
unusual sight, to say the least. Yet in 43 minutes, 1,070 people
strode by Joshua Bell without so much as a second glance.

I'm not saying Joshua Bell is God, mind you, but I do
think there are some compelling parallels in these two stories. There were seven people like Moses in the metro station
that day—seven people who stopped to bask in a moment of
rare beauty, seven people who listened and heard something
otherworldly in the notes streaming from Bell's violin that
morning. Most everyone else didn't even see the musician,
or if they did, they were too busy to stop, too busy to listen.

It's also important that we notice exactly when God spoke
to Moses:

> Moses saw that though the bush was on fire it did not burn
> up. So Moses thought, "I will go over and see this strange
> sight—why the bush does not burn up."

119

*When the LORD saw that he had gone over to look,* God called to him from within the bush, "Moses! Moses!"

And Moses said, "Here I am." (Exod. 3:2–4, emphasis mine)

> I wonder if God is calling us to the far side of the wilderness, so that we, like Moses, will hear God and see God and know that we are on holy ground.

God only spoke to Moses once Moses stopped to look. I wonder how many times we miss a sign or a call from God simply because we don't stop to look and listen. I wonder how often we fail to notice God's presence simply because we are distracted by the hustle of our everyday lives. I wonder if God is calling us to the far side of the wilderness, so that we, like Moses, will hear God and see God and know that we are on holy ground.

## Stand Still and See

The narrow road rose steeply in a series of switchbacks, the cliff plunging off a sheer precipice just beyond the flimsy guardrail. "I don't feel well," my son Noah said, his voice quavering from the backseat, his face pinched and gray beneath a sprinkling of freckles. We exited at the nearest pull-off. "Breathe in through your nose and out through your mouth, like this," I instructed, demonstrating the relaxation technique as we climbed out of the van and walked slowly up the worn stairs to the overlook. "The fresh air will help," I added, wrapping my arm around his shoulders.

We peered over the split-rail fence into the canyon, where white water raged thousands of feet below us. "I need to sit," Noah said, abruptly plunking onto a rotten log that had been shoved to the side of the trail. He looked worse, despite the deep breathing.

We sat for a long time in that spot. Brad and Rowan discovered a colony of carpenter ants beneath a layer of decaying bark. Noah breathed, battling nausea.

I, on the other hand, was agitated. After all, we were vacationing in Yellowstone, which meant we should have been glimpsing grizzly bears, roiling geysers, and sputtering fumaroles—at least *something* more dramatic than ants cavorting in a rotten log.

Restless and antsy (no pun intended)—How long does it take to recover from a bout of car sickness anyway?—I stood up and meandered down the trail to gaze into the canyon. It was during the second or third of these agitated wanderings that I spotted something moving in the distance, a flash of white against gray rock. It was a mother mountain goat and her two tiny young scrambling along the far side of the canyon—a rare sighting. I could hear the echo of rocks tumbling down the steep cliff as the young goats chased each other in and out of the shadows while their mother snatched mouthfuls of weeds.

Noah still didn't feel well enough to move, so the four of us watched the goats from our perch. We also spotted a woodpecker, barely visible in a nearby Douglas fir. With his brilliant yellow belly and black-and-white zebra plumage, he was unlike any woodpecker I'd ever seen in Nebraska.

"Stand still and see this great thing the LORD is about to do before your eyes!" the prophet Samuel urged the Israelites (1 Sam. 12:16). That's just it, of course. God is always doing something great before our eyes; his creation is always bursting into view before us; he is always present with us. But more often than not, we don't see him, simply because we don't stop to look—not in the bustling metro station, not in our own backyards, not even when we're on vacation— perhaps especially when we are on vacation.

That day several years ago when we sat on the edge of the trail in Yellowstone, I watched a steady stream of vacationers pass by and was struck by how little they appeared to notice their surroundings. None of the dozens of people who walked past us spotted the woodpecker, and few stayed long enough at the overlook to notice the agile goats (we pointed them out to those who lingered longer than a few seconds). Most of the tourists simply read the placard, snapped a photo or two of the canyon, and moved on, determined to reach their next destination and cross another Yellowstone highlight off their itineraries. Until the moment we were forced by Noah's car sickness to sit in one spot, we'd done exactly the same: racing through our vacation, hustling on to the next scenic spot, bent on maximizing our time.

Wherever we are and whatever we are doing, God invites us to the far side of the wilderness to commune with him. Saying yes to that invitation requires a willingness to step away from the noise, distractions, and demands of our daily life, at least for a little while. We needn't stay on the far side of the wilderness forever; given our many responsibilities, that's neither practical nor possible for most of us. Nor do we need to travel very far. The far side of my wilderness is a park bench at the edge of a little-traveled path. The far side of your wilderness might be a country dirt road, a winding trail through the forest, a patch of sand at the beach, or a quiet corner in your own backyard. Your far side of the wilderness could even be within the confines of your own home—a special armchair that you retreat to in the early morning hours or late in the evening, after your family has gone to bed. For me, personally, it helps to visit a physical location away from my own home, such as the park bench, because the place itself is a signal to my brain to settle into rest. But for you, the far side of the wilderness may, in fact, exist in the far reaches of your own mind—a place of quietness and solace you visit in meditation or contemplative prayer. As Thomas Merton said, "As soon as man is fully disposed to be alone with God, he is alone with God no matter where he may be—in the country, the monastery, the woods or the city."[1]

Many years after Moses first experienced God in the burning bush, he offered some words of advice to his fellow Israelites. Moses was an old man by this point, and, having just been informed by God that he was nearing the end of his life and would not cross the Jordan River to step into the Promised Land alongside his people, he was compelled to preach a final sermon to those who would go on ahead without him. Eugene Peterson notes that this sermon in Deuteronomy (Deut. 1–33) is the longest sermon in the Bible and perhaps the longest sermon ever, and in many ways, it's what you might expect from a successful leader's final words: wise, insightful, and firm.

Moses recaps the Israelites' story from captivity in Egypt through their forty years of wandering in the wilderness, and he reminds his people of God's commands as well as God's promises. As I read through Deuteronomy recently, though, I couldn't help but notice how often Moses also repeatedly urges the Israelites to stay alert and watchful. "Pay attention. . . . Just make sure you stay alert. . . . Don't forget anything of what you've seen. . . . Stay vigilant as long as you live" (Deut. 4:5, 9

Message). This is the man whose willingness to stop, look, and notice his surroundings alerted him to the presence of God. Here, in his final words to his people, we see him urging them to keep the same kind of attentiveness and watchfulness, so that they too would be aware of God's presence in their midst.

Moses' last words to his people are meant for us as well. Pay attention. Stay alert. Be vigilant. God is here with us, just as he promised. But sometimes we must go to the far side of the wilderness to sense his presence. Sometimes we must stand still in order to see the great things God is doing right before our very eyes.

### We Are Not Privy to God's Plan

Still, it needs to be said here: the wilderness isn't always all frolicking mountain goats and brightly colored woodpeckers, and answering God's invitation into the far side of the wilderness doesn't always lead to a burning bush. Sometimes when we step into the wilderness, all we see ahead is vast emptiness, the unknown, an unmarked path. "My Lord God, I have no idea where I am going," Thomas Merton wrote. "I do not see the road ahead of me. I cannot know for sure where it will end. Nor do I really know myself, and the fact that I think I am following your will does not mean that I am actually doing so."[2] This is the wilderness experience.

Many years ago, long before our children were born, my husband and I backpacked through a small section of Yellowstone National Park. I'd reluctantly agreed to this adventure, knowing that Old Faithful Inn—or any place with plumbing, for that matter—suited me better. A twenty-five-pound pack and a two-man tent pitched on pine cones was not my idea of vacation. But I had agreed, largely because I was newly married and still very much in the "I'll do anything for you" stage.

On our first day out, Brad and I hiked through a barren landscape, charred husks of birch and pine standing like totems, the ground prickly with new-growth brush. A rampant forest fire had ravaged that part of the park a few years prior, and the burned landscape was still as stark and desolate as a moonscape.

As morning turned to noon and the sun grew hot, the pack straps began to burn ruts into my shoulders, my fancy hiking boots chafed blisters on my heels, and my hair stuck to the nape of my neck like strands of overcooked spaghetti. Weary of the ugly, sooty landscape, I became crankier with each mile. As we rounded each rise I expected to glimpse our final destination in the distance: a lush valley, a glinting lake, our campsite nestled into the cool shade. Instead, at the crest of each hill I saw only another rise ahead, the hope of shade and rest and refreshing water fading as one false summit gave way to the next.

"I really want to be there now," I complained mercilessly to Brad. "How much farther? When are we going to see the campsite? Why are there so many hills?"

"This is horrible!" I continued. "This isn't what I expected at all! It's too hard! I'm not having fun!"

Every time I read about the Israelites' wilderness wandering I can't help but remember that terrible Yellowstone hike. My time in the wilderness was comparatively short (a mere day and a night compared to the Israelites' forty years), but in those hours, time slowed to a crawl. The journey was longer, the terrain rougher, and the circumstances more challenging than I had anticipated. The trail was neither straight nor flat, I couldn't see our final destination, and, several miles into the journey, I seriously began to question my husband's navigational skills. Like the Israelites, I complained bitterly and doubted my leader. All hope of ever reaching the promised land vanished, and I lamented the fact that I had ever left the comfort of the lodge and embarked on the hike in the first place.

During their forty years in the wilderness, the Israelites traveled with God as their guide. During the day, God went ahead of the Israelites in a pillar of cloud, and at night in a pillar of fire to give them light (see Exod. 13:20–22). God never left his people alone, yet at the same time, he also didn't tell them much about his game plan. In fact, the Bible tells us that at one point, God didn't lead his people on the shortest, most obvious route, but instead, guided them on a more circuitous path around the desert and toward the Red Sea (see Exod. 13:17–18).

We, as twenty-first-century readers of the Bible, know that God had a very good reason for leading his people along this longer, roundabout route: "For God said, 'If they face war, they might change their minds and return to Egypt'" (Exod. 13:17). The Bible tells us God's reasoning; but God didn't tell the Israelites. We can see that in making them travel a greater distance, God was actually protecting the Israelites. He knew they were in a fragile state and couldn't handle going to war. But the Israelites themselves were not privy to this insider information. They simply followed the pillar of cloud and the pillar of fire regardless of whether it led them on a longer, more circuitous route or not. They could not see or understand that God was in fact looking out for their best interests by making them go the longer way.

I never expected that a descent into the dark night of the soul would be a critical part of my spiritual journey toward wholeness. I also didn't anticipate that descent would take place on a spiritual retreat in one of the most serene, idyllic places I'd ever been. In fact, I had hoped for the opposite: I thought I might achieve some sort of spiritual breakthrough (in retrospect, it was a breakthrough . . . just not the kind I'd imagined). And I certainly never expected that confronting my deepest brokenness would, ironically and paradoxically, bring me to a deeper knowledge of myself and a more authentic connection with God. I never saw any of that coming. When I was in the midst of the descent and the subsequent wilderness wandering that followed, I couldn't see the way through. I could not see the road ahead, and I could not see God.

We often can't understand why God appears to make our journey longer or more difficult than it needs to be. We can't see when or how he is protecting us and loving us in his "no," or in his "stay," or in his "walk this longer way." We are not privy to the big picture. God knows the route that is best for us, but we can't always see the way ourselves. As my friend Deidra says, "God is always working upstream." The catch is, it takes a while for the current to carry the results of God's work to us.

## You Must Lose Your Life

As I mentioned earlier, a gardener will usually make the first and most drastic pruning cuts on a tree during autumn, or even, depending on the climate, during the winter, when the tree is in its dormant phase. During these quiet months, the tree is not expending energy to move sugars and water up

127

and down its trunk and out to its branches and leaves, and therefore it can focus on resting and healing from the wounds the gardener inflicts during the pruning process.

Allowing God to cut away the false parts of ourselves is a wounding of sorts. He may be pruning away aspects of ourselves that are unnecessary or even threatening to our true selves, but the cutting stings nonetheless. In the pruning we lose parts of our identities that we've long clung to, perhaps even pieces of ourselves with which we've identified and which we have long allowed to define us. The fact that these are not the best, most fruitful pieces of ourselves doesn't mean it won't hurt to let them go, nor does it mean we won't be afraid to release them. As our limbs and branches tumble to the ground, we struggle to recognize and redefine the bare, exposed, vulnerable self that remains.

Jesus said to his disciples, "For whoever wants to save their life will lose it, but whoever loses their life for me will save it. What good will it be for someone to gain the whole world, yet forfeit their soul? Or what can anyone give in exchange for their soul?" (Matt. 16:25–26). It's significant that Jesus' statement is repeated almost verbatim in all three of the synoptic Gospels (see also Mark 8:35–37 and Luke 9:24–25). *Pay attention to this*, Mark, Matthew, and Luke are saying in unison. Barbara Brown Taylor points out that the Greek word for "life" used in these passages is *psyche*—meaning the human breath, life, or soul. "While Greek has no word for 'ego,' psyche comes close," Taylor explains. "The salvation of the psyche begins with its own demise."[3]

This all sounds good and right when Barbara Brown Taylor says it or when we read it in the Bible, but the truth is, losing your life in order to save it is hard work. Our natural

inclination as human beings is to clutch something with all
our might. We don't release easily; we don't give up easily;
we don't lose easily. It is uncomfortable, often painful work
to give up the identity we have so carefully crafted. There is
a real sense of loss in the process.

I imagine the Israelites must have felt something similar
after their exodus from Egypt. Living under the tyranny of
the Egyptians for hundreds of years, their identity as individuals and as a people was undoubtedly shaped by their history as slaves. Emerging free and unfettered from Egypt, they
would have had an awful lot to let go of—fear, anger, grief,
bitterness—and a lot of personal, emotional, and spiritual
rebuilding to do. They would have had a lot to learn about
themselves and about God.

This is why, when the going got tough out in the wilderness, the Israelites clamored to return to their former lives
of enslavement back in Egypt. As painful and terrible as
life was in Egypt, at least it was familiar. At least they recognized themselves there. At least they had an identity they
understood there. It's no wonder God had the Israelites stay
in the wilderness for forty years. God's people needed every
bit of that time to lean into the slow, laborious work of healing in order to live into their true identity. In our journey
toward uncovering and living into our true selves, we need
that time too.

Like the Israelites who were liberated from Egypt only to
wander in the wilderness, we, too, enter an in-between time,
a quiet period after the hard prune but before the regrowth.
Like a tree that has been radically pruned, we have wounded
places that are now raw and exposed. We can see more clearly
into the center of ourselves, and we may not recognize or

even like what is there. We wait for the slow healing, the slow revealing. As Sue Monk Kidd says, "We posture ourselves in ways that allow God to heal, transform and create us."[4] This, too, is the wilderness experience.

Several years ago the bishop of the Nebraska synod of my Lutheran denomination preached at my church, and a few minutes into his sermon on the book of Numbers, he said something I have never forgotten: "The wilderness," the bishop said, "is the place God's people stay and wait while God is up to something his people can't possibly see or even imagine."

I heard the bishop make that statement about the wilderness three times that Sunday. Because I was participating in the liturgy, I sat through all three worship services, something I'd never done before. And every time I heard the bishop make that declaration about the wilderness, I nodded my head yes. Before I left the sanctuary that day, I jotted his words onto my bulletin and slipped it into my purse. I couldn't have said why at the time, but I knew they were words I didn't want to forget.

> "The wilderness," the bishop said, "is the place God's people stay and wait while God is up to something his people can't possibly see or even imagine."

Five days later my agent called to tell me my publisher had turned down my proposal for a second book. Sales for my first book were weak, and as a result, the publishing house had to let me go. Over the next few weeks, the same proposal was turned down by nearly a dozen more publishers. In a matter of a few short weeks, my professional life tanked. My dream of continuing to write and publish books had come up against a major roadblock, and I was roiling in the throes of depression, resentment, fear, and anger . . . mostly anger. I blamed God for leading me down the publishing road, only to bring me to what looked like a definitive dead end. In short, I found myself deep in what was beginning to feel like an unrelenting wilderness. Turns out, the bishop's words only sounded good when I wasn't actually *in* the wilderness. In reality, there's not much to like about the concepts "stay and wait" and "can't see or possibly imagine" when you're smack in the middle of the wilderness with no clear way out.

One morning, as I was still wrestling through this period of figuring out who I was and what I should do with my life, Brad stopped to talk to me as I sat slumped on the couch. "You know that verse you have posted over the bathroom sink, the one about God's promise?" he asked. I nodded. I knew the one. It was Hebrews 10:23: "Let us hold tightly without wavering to the hope we affirm, for God can be trusted to keep his promise" (NLT). I'd read it over and over, every time I washed my hands, every time I brushed my teeth, every time I touched up my lipstick or applied mascara. I knew the words by heart because I was banking on that promise.

"The thing is, hon," Brad continued gently, "God's promise doesn't necessarily include another book deal."

I can't even begin to tell you how angry I was at my husband in that moment—mostly because I knew he was right.

In that moment I realized it was true: God had never promised me another book deal. In fact, he hadn't promised the first book deal. He didn't promise that I'd get to spend my whole professional career as an author. He didn't promise me a particular job, even if it was a job I was passionate about and to which I felt called. The truth is, God doesn't promise to give us the job we desire, the spouse we yearn for, the baby we so desperately want, or the medical test results we are praying for. He doesn't promise us wealth, health, success, an easy road, or even happiness. In fact, God doesn't promise to give us most of what we think we want or even most of what we think we need.

This is hard to accept, especially when you've been dropped into the middle of the wilderness, facing the job loss, your spouse's terminal diagnosis, your daughter's drug addiction, the infertility, the discouraging PET scan results, the notice of foreclosure. This is hard to accept when the way through is neither straight nor clear. It's hard to accept when there's no burning bush, no pillars of cloud or flame. Yet at the same time, God's promise couldn't be more straightforward. "I am with you always," Jesus said, "even to the end of the age" (Matt. 28:20 NLT). God makes other promises in the Bible—he promises eternal life, for instance (see 1 John 2:25), and a new heart and spirit (see Ezek. 36:26)—but those promises essentially point to the same, foundational promise Jesus made to his disciples and to us, which is this: I will be with you always, no matter what.

It's no coincidence God had me sit through the bishop's sermon three times in a single Sunday. I am willful and stubborn and spiritually hard of hearing. God knows I need to hear a message more than once for it to stick. God also knew that five days from that Sunday morning I would find myself in the wilderness and would need a reminder of what I was supposed to do there.

Four years later, I'm still thinking about the bishop's definition of the wilderness, particularly about those two small but important words: *stay* and *wait*. I don't know about you, but to me *stay* and *wait* are two of the least appealing words in the English language, especially when you find yourself in a place where the path is neither straight nor clear and all you want is out. But the truth is, staying and waiting are two of the most fundamental aspects of the journey toward uncovering our true selves. God calls us to stay and wait, and all the while, he is working out something we can't see or even imagine.

## GOING DEEPER

Jesus himself was led by the Holy Spirit into the wilderness, where he faced physical and spiritual temptation and undoubtedly wrestled with loneliness and isolation during his forty days of solitude (see Luke 4:1–13). The wilderness is a formidable place, and yet, like Jesus and like the Israelites, we are intentionally led there by God to be both refined and sustained. The wilderness is also the place where, distanced from distraction and noise, we hear God speak tenderly to us as he leads us through the dense bramble and out the other side.

Here are some questions to consider for times when the path ahead is unclear:

1. Where is your "far side of the wilderness"—the place you are most able to stand still to experience the presence of God? If you don't have such a place, can you think

of a spot you can retreat to—a bench, a path through the woods, a quiet corner of your house—that's free of distraction and noise?

2. Have you considered that God could be intentionally leading you to the far side of the wilderness for a particular reason? What might he be yearning for you to see or hear as you stand still?

3. Jesus willingly followed the Holy Spirit into the wilderness. The Israelites willingly followed Moses into the wilderness, but later resisted God's call to continue the journey through the desert. Who are you in the midst of your wilderness journey—a willing or a resistant follower? If you find yourself resistant, can you identify what you are resisting and why?

4. What have you wanted or expected from God that is not, in fact, something he has promised you?

# 7

# rooted

## Practicing the discipline of staying in place

> The day came when the risk to remain tight in
> a bud was more painful than the risk it took to
> blossom.
>
> —Anais Nin

Back when we were dating, Brad entrusted me with his favorite plant, a lush ficus tree named Herman (in honor of
Herman Melville; it's true . . . I married a man whose favorite book is *Moby Dick*) before he left town for an extended
period. I moved Herm into my parents' house, where I was
living at the time, positioned him next to the sliding glass
doors, and gave him a satisfying drink from the watering can.
Two days later I discovered a number of Herm's leaves had
yellowed and dropped onto the floor. Thinking that perhaps

he wasn't getting enough sunlight, I moved him to a south-facing window. The next morning more leaves littered the carpet. I fed Herm some plant food and repositioned him yet again in a less drafty spot in the house. Still he dropped leaves.

A week after Brad left, I called him to report that I'd killed Herman the Ficus in a record-setting seven days flat. That's when Brad mentioned the one detail he'd neglected to tell me before he'd left town. Turns out, ficus plants don't like to be moved around. They thrive best when they stay in one place.

When they first join the order, Benedictine monks and nuns take a vow of stability. "The vow of stability affirms sameness," explains author and Episcopal priest Elizabeth Canham, "a willingness to attend to the present moment, to the reality of this place, these people, as God's gift to me and the setting where I live out my discipleship."[1] To "affirm sameness" is radically countercultural in our society. We are conditioned, even encouraged, to drop one thing and move on to the next. We update our résumés when we find ourselves bored on the job. We buy a new pair of shoes when we see the toes are scuffed on the pair we are wearing. We unfriend the acquaintance on Facebook when her political views contrast with ours. We upgrade to the new iPhone when the version we own still runs just fine. We abandon with ease, enticed by the fresh and new.

Yet it's clear this relentless pursuit of the perfect place, the perfect situation, the perfect job, and the perfect person often leads to the Herman the Ficus phenomenon: in moving from place to place, thing to thing, and person to person, we end up feeling restless, uprooted, and displaced. Constant change and transition leave us withered and exhausted. Like Herm the Ficus, in our constant motion we begin to lose important pieces of ourselves. We begin to fall apart.

Turns out, Herm wasn't dead, though he certainly looked it. After I called Brad with the bad news, I stopped moving Herm around the house and let him be. I was too lazy to lug him downstairs and toss him into the trash bin, so he stood neglected, spindly, and nude in a corner of the living room. A few weeks passed. And then one day, as I was walking by, I saw something that stopped me in my tracks. Tiny buds dotted every one of Herm's bare branches. Unnoticed by me in the weeks since I'd written him off as dead, Herm had begun to thrive, unfurling leaf by delicate leaf until finally, months after Brad had left him with me, Herm was once again a lush, verdant ficus. Brad had been right. Herm had simply needed to stay in one place. Left in the same spot, he grew strong and whole once again.

## Plan to Stay

In February 2015 the Bible Lands Museum in Jerusalem exhibited a never-before-seen collection of more than 100 clay tablets dating back to between 572 and 477 BCE. The tablets, written in the Babylonian language in cuneiform script, were discovered in what's now Iraq. They are considered by historians to be direct evidence of the Jewish community that was established in Babylonia following King Nebuchadnezzar's invasion of Judea and his destruction of the temple in 600 BCE. Filip Vukosavovic, the exhibition's curator, said studying the tablets was "like hitting the jackpot. We started reading the tablets and within minutes we were absolutely stunned," he said. "It fills in a critical gap in understanding what was going on in the life of Judeans in Babylonia more than 2,500 years ago."[2]

The information written on the tablets is surprisingly ordinary, even mundane: details of retail transactions for the purchase of animals and produce; records of paid taxes, debts owed, and credits accumulated; marriage deeds; lease agreements; partnership contracts; slave sales; inheritance documents; and other financial and legal notes. "On the one hand it's boring details," said Vukosavovic, "but on the other you learn so much about who these exiled people were and how they lived."[3] In short, what the tablets convey is that the Israelites were going about their business, living richly and abundantly even while in exile. They thrived, even as they stayed in one place in less-than-ideal circumstances and waited on God. The ancient texts also confirm that the Israelites listened to and obeyed God's instructions laid out by the prophet Jeremiah:

> Build homes and plan to stay. Plant gardens, and eat the food they produce. Marry and have children. Then find spouses for them so that you may have many grandchildren. Multiply! Do not dwindle away! And work for the peace and prosperity of the city where I sent you into exile. (Jer. 29:5–7 NLT)

The Israelites spent seventy long years exiled in Babylon, nearly twice the time they wandered in the wilderness after their exodus from Egypt. Babylon was another wilderness of sorts, but this time, they were not called to move forward, but to stay—and not only to stay, but to live their lives, to put down roots, and to make this new, unfamiliar place their home, a place where there was the potential to grow and thrive. The ancient tablets discovered 2,500 years after their exile confirm that the Israelites did exactly that. Led into a second wilderness in Babylonian exile, the Israelites stayed and built a life for themselves with God's blessing. Meanwhile, God was up to something they couldn't possibly see or even imagine.

Sometimes, like the Israelites in Babylon, God calls us into the wilderness and asks us to stay right where we are. Here we practice the spiritual discipline of stability. Episcopal priest and author Jane Tomaine notes that the words *stable* and *stability* come from the Latin word *stare*, meaning to stand or to be still. From this, she explains, "comes the figurative meaning to be firm, to stand fast, to endure, to persevere, to be rooted." In other words, "stability is the action of staying put, remaining steadfast and faithful to the situation in which God has placed us."[4] In Babylon, God grew the Israelites' perseverance, resilience, steadfastness, and, above all, their trust. As they stayed in place, putting down roots, growing, and thriving, they rediscovered who they were as a people chosen and loved by God. Babylon wasn't a perfect or an ideal situation, and it certainly wasn't the Israelites' first choice, but God sustained them there and grew their faith.

Of course, staying put is a lot easier when you are in a place you actually want to be. Ask me to stay put on a Caribbean beach with a good novel in one hand and a piña colada in the other, and I'm there, fully engaged and thriving, no problem. But what happens when we are asked to stay in a place we don't particularly like, a place that's hard, a place that's not comfortable or fulfilling? What happens when we are asked to stay and wait in a barren desert, a wasteland, a place that feels like stagnation?

Such was the case after the proposal for my second book was turned down. As weeks turned to months, and I found myself spinning my wheels in a place of professional and vocational uncertainty, I couldn't help but wonder why God was not making a definitive path clear. *Should I update my résumé and begin applying for jobs in the traditional workplace again?* I wondered. *Should I come up with a different book idea and write a new proposal? Should I focus on freelancing and pitch a bunch of article ideas to websites and magazines? Or should I try a little bit of everything and see what sticks?* I wanted to *do* something, anything . . . the problem was, I wasn't at all sure what it was I should do.

When I was a kid, my dad offered my sister and me one particular piece of advice again and again, especially when we found ourselves facing a difficult decision. "When in conflict, do nothing," he repeated to us time and time again at various points in our lives. I was never especially fond of this advice. First of all, it was in direct opposition to his other favorite mantra—"Make it happen"—so I was never sure when it was time to "make it happen" versus when it was time to "do nothing." As a triple-type-A go-getter, I tended to land squarely in the "make it happen" camp and was much less comfortable with the "do nothing" stance.

As I've matured, I am more able to see the wisdom in my dad's "do nothing" advice, though admittedly, I struggle to follow it in the midst of my own periods of conflict and indecision. I think my dad was essentially promoting the concept of stability and steadfastness in the face of uncertainty, which doesn't necessarily imply doing nothing, per se, but simply suggests we adopt a listening stance rather than steamrolling forward in full-blown panic. Unfortunately, I usually choose the second of the two approaches.

Case in point: In the weeks and months after the proposal for my second book was turned down by publishers across the board, I concocted a number of plans and expectations related to how I thought the pieces of my fragmented career should fall into place. When there appeared to be movement in any particular direction, I ran with it, confident that a door was opening, confident that I knew God's plan for me.

*Aha!* I would declare to myself every time a glimmer of hope appeared on the horizon. *So THIS is what God's going to do. THIS is how it's all going to work out!* I was so sure I knew what God was going to do, so sure I could predict his plans for me. Until, that is, God didn't do what I expected at all, and I found myself back at square one—still with no publisher, a whole lot of questions, and no clear career direction.

I cycled through this process of planning, expectations, hope, and disappointment three separate times over a period of two months before I finally realized something important: God hadn't failed me, and he hadn't intentionally led me down dead-end paths. The fact was, it wasn't God who had created any of those plans in the first place. It was me. They were *my* plans. I put my faith, hope, and confidence in Plans A, B, and C—plans of my own making—instead of in God himself. Instead of leaning into a steadfast stance of listening and waiting, I had created my own plans, called them God's, and them blamed God when my plans didn't work out as I had anticipated.

The truth is, we like details; we like a clear plan. Even Moses asked God for specifics. Frustrated with his people and disappointed in his own leadership skills, Moses laid it on the line with God: "You have been telling me, 'Take these people up to the Promised Land.' But you haven't told me whom you will send with me," Moses complained. "You have told me, 'I know you by name, and I look favorably on you.' If it is true that you look favorably on me, let me know your ways, so I may understand you more fully and continue to enjoy your favor" (Exod. 33:12–13 NLT).

Moses demanded specifics—"Whom will you send with me?"—as well as a clear plan—"Teach me your ways." But that's not what God offered him as an answer. "I will personally go with you, Moses, and I will give you rest—everything will be fine for you," God replied (Exod. 33:14 NLT). Like Moses, we want to know the plan; we want specifics—the who, what, why, and when. But God gives us something better: his presence. God is who he says he is: Emmanuel—God *with* us. As God tells Aaron in the Old Testament, "I am your plot of ground" (Num. 18:20 Message). It's not about the plan; it's not about the specifics; it's not about the land or the inheritance or what we get. It's about God in us and with us, and us with him and in him.

"For I know the plans I have for you," says the Lord, "plans to prosper you and not harm you, plans to give you hope and a future" (Jer. 29:11). Notice the wording here. It's not, "For *you* know the plans I have for you" or even "For I will tell you the plans I have for you." It's very clear who God considers the master planner and who he intends as the followers here. We don't always get to know God's plans, and even when we do get an inkling of what God has in store for us, it's likely not what we had in mind for ourselves.

When the Israelites heard they were to spend seventy years in exile before being brought home (in this case God actually did lay out the big picture plan for them in advance; see Jer. 29:10), they were undoubtedly frustrated and disappointed. Seventy years is a long time—a lifetime for most people. And yet as the ancient clay tablets reveal, the Israelites listened to and obeyed God's commands, trusting that he had their best interests in mind. They built homes. They planted gardens. They married and had children and grandchildren. In short, they stayed in one place and made the best of it until God told them it was time to move.

### Prayerful Expectancy

We typically think of the Old Testament when we hear the word *wilderness*, but there are plenty of examples of staying and waiting in the New Testament too. The Gospel of Luke tells the story of a man named Simeon in Jerusalem who was called to wait. The Holy Spirit had revealed to Simeon that he would not die until he had seen the Messiah, and so Simeon bided his time, "eagerly waiting for the Messiah to come and rescue Israel" (Luke 2:25 NLT).

Luke doesn't offer any details about Simeon's waiting period, nor does he tell us how much Simeon knew about the coming Messiah. Nevertheless, I picture Simeon as an old man, patiently waiting in the "prayerful expectancy" (as *The Message* puts it) of hope for Israel. I'm also guessing he probably didn't expect the Messiah to show up as an infant. Yet Simeon waited, steadfast and faithful, even when he didn't have a complete picture of who he was waiting for.

Finally, led by the Holy Spirit to the temple on the day of Jesus' circumcision, Simeon spotted Mary and Joseph. Taking the infant Jesus in his arms, Simeon thanked and praised God, saying, "Sovereign Lord, now let your servant die in peace, as you have promised. I have seen your salvation, which you have prepared for all people" (Luke 2:29–31 NLT).

I can't imagine that the kind of waiting Simeon endured was fun. I wonder, did he get discouraged? Did he ever doubt he had heard the Holy Spirit correctly? For a long time there was no evidence that what the Holy Spirit had told him was true. Was Simeon ever mocked for his faith, which may have looked to others like foolishness or even laziness? The text doesn't tell us, but my guess is, it wasn't always easy for Simeon to wait in prayerful expectancy. And yet, that's exactly what he did. Day after day, year after year, Simeon stayed and waited, trusting in steadfast faith that God was up to something he couldn't see or possibly imagine.

Likewise, in that same chapter of Luke's Gospel, we read about the prophetess Anna, who on the day of Jesus' circumcision was also biding her time in the temple. Anna, the text tells us, was long-widowed and hadn't left the temple since her husband's death eighty-four years prior. She stayed there day and night, worshiping, fasting, and praying. Anna was waiting too, and when she spotted Mary and Joseph with the infant Jesus, like Simeon, she immediately began to praise God. "She talked about the child to everyone who had been *waiting expectantly* for God to rescue Jerusalem" (Luke 2:38 NLT, emphasis mine).

*Prayerful expectancy. Waiting expectantly.* The word *expectant* or *expect* comes from the Latin words *ex* ("out") and *spectare* ("to look at"). To be expectant means to look out for or await, which is exactly what Simeon and Anna were doing in the temple all those years. They stayed in place, watching and waiting with expectant hope for the presence of God to pass by. Simeon and Anna waited nearly their whole lives for Christ to reveal himself. Day after day, they consistently showed up to the same place to wait in expectant hope for the fulfillment of God's promise. Simeon and Anna embodied the very definition of faith as described in Hebrews: "confidence in what we hope for and assurance about what we do not see" (11:1).

The practice of open center pruning often takes up to three years, with long periods of rest and waiting between pruning sessions. Japanese gardener Jake Hobson notes that after a hard prune, a tree's trunk is often wrapped in burlap to protect the newly revealed and tender bark from the elements during the recovery and resting period.[5] During this time, the gardener watches the tree, waiting for healing and the slow results of transformation to be revealed.

Deep, radical transformation does not take place overnight. It is a slow process, requiring time for healing, waiting, listening, watching, resting, and recovery. Like a pruned tree, our souls need this time. Staying in place, especially when we'd rather be moving forward or climbing upward, is a difficult but necessary part of deep soul work. Most of us are probably more comfortable with the "make it happen" mode, rather than the "do nothing" mode. But we can't rush through the staying and waiting in order to hurry on to growth and transformation.

The Benedictines call this slow, transformative work *conversatio morum*—"conversion of life." As Elizabeth Canham says, "The monk realizes he is not yet fully the person God created him to be, that he is on the way to knowing himself as one loved and created in the divine image whose call is to be as Christ in the world but who has not yet arrived."[6] Sometimes, even as we are in the midst of uncovering our truest self, we are called to stay right where we are. Not-yet-there is not a perfect place, nor is it always a comfortable place, but it's an important place. Like the nine-month gestation period of a pregnancy, a soul waits for its time to arrive.

> Not-yet-there is not a perfect place, nor is it always a comfortable place, but it's an important place.

## Let Yourself Be Looked Upon

In the hours and days following my descent into the dark night of the soul in Tuscany, I struggled with a host of new and unfamiliar emotions. Unable to avoid the knowledge and insights that had been revealed to me, I was forced to sit with the pain, grief, and fear that had risen unbridled to the surface. I looked and acted "normal" on the outside— I participated in the conversations, excursions, meals, and companionship of my fellow travelers—but all the while I was reeling on the inside with questions and uncertainty. There was no opportunity to flee from or press back the discomfort. I was forced to face it head-on and stay present to it.

Each morning that week, Jamin sent us back out into the garden, armed with our journals, Scripture, and questions for reflection, and each morning I picked up my wrestling match with God where I'd left off the day before. The subsequent matches weren't, thankfully, nearly as wrenching as that initial descent on Sunday morning. This was a quieter, more contemplative wrestling, a reckoning of sorts. God had led me into a new, unfamiliar, disconcerting place, and there I stayed—quiet, observant, waiting.

Each morning I sought the same spot, retreating to a secluded bench tucked under an arbor. Hidden by a veil of flowering vines, I could see into the garden, but with my knees pulled to my chest, I was almost entirely out of sight. I felt the need to be small and hidden, and the bench under the arbor became my hiding place.

I didn't journal much during my forty-five minutes or so at the bench, nor did I spend much time reflecting on the questions and prompts for the day. Instead, each morning I sat with my back against the cool stone wall. I listened to the sound of water splashing into a nearby fountain, the sleepy drone of bees nosing into lavender, a rooster crowing on the other side of the wall. I breathed in the scent of jasmine and felt the warm breeze on my face. I observed tiny emerald lizards emerge from beneath the shrubs to bask, unaware of my presence, on the sun-warmed paving stones. I watched light dapple the leaves, heat shimmer in the distance, and clouds skitter across the sky.

"Attentiveness is vital to waiting," says Sue Monk Kidd. She points out that the word *wait* comes from a root word meaning "to watch." "Originally to wait meant to apply attentiveness or watchfulness throughout a period of time," she adds in her book *When the Heart Waits*. "To wait on God meant to watch keenly for God's coming."[7] This is what Simeon and Anna were doing in the temple day in and day out as they waited for the Messiah's arrival. And although I didn't entirely realize it at the time, this is what I was doing those mornings in the garden, hidden beneath the arbor with my back against the cool stone. I was watching, and in my watching, I was waiting on God. It was during those mornings of watchful, attentive waiting that I began, ever so slowly, to awaken to both God's presence and to his personal invitation to me.

"Find a quiet, secluded place so you won't be tempted to role-play before God," advised Matthew in his Gospel. "Just be there as simply and honestly as you can manage. The focus will shift from you to God, and you will begin to sense his grace" (Matt. 6:6 Message). During those mornings in the garden, I finally stopped role-playing before God. Stripped of my leaves and branches, I was my whole self, my deepest brokenness and my deepest desires exposed. "Can you let God 'look upon you in your lowliness,' as Mary put it in Luke 1:48, without waiting for some future moment when you believe you are worthy?" asks Richard Rohr.[8] Those mornings in the garden I let God see me, to look upon me in my lowliness, brokenness, and despair, and in doing so, I began to see myself not as I always had, as a producer and a striver and an achiever, but in a new way, as a new creation. Ever so slowly during those watchful mornings hidden in the garden, I began to see and know myself as beloved.

## This Is My Beloved

A few weeks ago I stood in church and sang the lyrics of a song that went like this: "If anybody asks you who I am, who I am, who I am . . . If anybody asks you who I am, say that I'm a child of God." Most of us equate "who I am" with "what I do." It's often the first question we ask a stranger when we are making small talk, right? "So, what do you do?" This is how society defines us and often how we define ourselves. We are what we do—accountant, nurse, professor, writer, mother, father. But this is not how God sees us and defines us. Like the song says, God identifies us as his children. Our primary identity—really, our only true identity—is beloved child of God.

Do you remember what God said after Jesus emerged from the Jordan River, having just been baptized by John the Baptist? As water streamed off Jesus' body, the heavens opened, the Spirit of God descended and settled on him, and a voice boomed down, saying, "This is my beloved Son, in whom I am well pleased" (Matt. 3:17 KJV). In that moment God named and identified Jesus as his beloved Son.

The thing is—and maybe this is true for you too—until recently I'd always considered that identifier, "beloved," unique to Jesus. It made sense to me that God would identify Jesus, his own Son, as his Beloved. Yet I never considered that I am given the same identity—beloved daughter. In fact, I used to roll my eyes at the parts of John's Gospel in which he refers to himself not once but *six times* as "the disciple whom Jesus loved" (see John 13:23; 19:26; 20:2, 8; 21:7, 20). *Who does that?* I always thought when I came across that phrase. *What an egomaniac!*

It's only recently that I realized John referred to himself as "the disciple whom Jesus loved" not because he was egotistical or a braggart, but because that was his primary identity: "loved by Jesus" was how John knew and defined himself. John believed in the deepest center of himself that he was first and foremost loved by God. And it was that belief and trust that allowed John to experience the deepest intimacy with Christ.

God desires that each one of us would know ourselves first and foremost as the beloved daughter or son of Christ. "Beloved" is not an identity unique to God's own son or to Jesus' favorite disciple. There are not a precious select few who earn the distinction of beloved. Beloved is the identity given to each one of us long before we enter this world as infants, even long before the universe itself was created, and our beloved-ness has nothing to do with whether we merit that distinction or not. Once we understand, accept, and embrace with our whole hearts and minds that we are beloved, period, everything else either falls away or falls into place.

> Once we understand, accept, and embrace with our whole hearts and minds that we are beloved, period, everything else either falls away or falls into place.

"It's in Christ we find out who we are and what we are living for" (Eph. 1:11 Message). How do you know who you are? By who God is and by who God says you are. God is Creator. God is love. God is everything. God is in everything (see Col. 1:16–17). And therefore God is in you. His love is in you, and you are defined principally by that love. This is how we understand and know ourselves: created by God, made in the image of God, embodiment of God, beloved of God.

Thinking back to my time in Tuscany, I'm not surprised God used his creation to invite me into deeper intimacy with him. I've always been happiest outdoors, whether I am sitting on the rocky lip of Lake Superior, standing amid the blowing

Bluestem tallgrass of the vast plains, or perched on a park bench at the far side of my own small wilderness. Nature has always been the place that frees me to be my truest self and the place I most often sense God's presence. Those days in Tuscany, particularly the mornings in the garden following my plummet into the dark night of the soul, were God's personal invitation to me to know him and love him and to be known by him and loved by him. The Tuscan garden was where I first truly began to understand what it means to be a child of God, God's Beloved, and why that understanding is the beginning of everything.

The first morning I tucked myself into the arbor, I noticed a tiny bud buried deep in the vines, a waxy pink fist clenched closed. The next day during my time at the bench, I saw that the bud had cracked open, four stiff, triangular petals split in a crosshatch to reveal a ball of tender inner pink petals, still folded tightly inside. The following morning, the bud was opened further yet, until finally, on my last morning in Tuscany, I saw that the bud was in full bloom, a ruffle of coral petals like a flamenco dancer's skirt encircling a multitude of bright yellow filament.

Each morning I sat under the arbor I snapped a photo of that single flower as it cracked further open, revealing its innermost center a little bit more each day as it transformed from bud to bloom. I knew there was a message for me in that tiny flower. I was still tender, still raw and exposed, reeling from what God had revealed to me in my dark night of the soul. I was still confused in my faith, confused by what I believed. But there was hope in that one small bud, once tightly closed, now opening bit by bit. I, too, had cracked open on the hillside Sunday morning, and in the days that followed, watching, waiting, and attentive in the cool shade of the arbor, I began to unfurl.

"It takes great trust to believe in the smallest of beginnings," Ann Voskamp writes in *The Broken Way*.[9] Those mornings in the garden were the smallest beginnings for me, but more than the garden and the place itself, it was the ample silence and solitude that offered a way into beginning to understand myself as God's Beloved. As Brennan Manning acknowledged, "The indispensable conditions for developing and maintaining the awareness of our belovedness is time alone with God. There we discover that the truth of our belovedness is really true. Our identity rests in God's relentless tenderness for us revealed in Jesus Christ."[10]

God leads us into the wilderness, where he speaks tenderly to us, his Beloved (see Hosea 2:14). There in the wilderness we stay and wait. Sometimes there is work to be done in our waiting; we are called to build houses and plant gardens. Sometimes, like Simeon and Anna, we wait in the midst of the everyday, prayerfully expectant, steadfastly hopeful. Sometimes we are still in our waiting—watchful, attentive, trusting . . . believing in the smallest beginnings.

## GOING DEEPER

*Conversatio morum*—conversion of life—is a long, slow process that often includes periods of what feels like indefinite waiting. Though we can't always discern it, God is at work, even in this season that looks like dormancy. Like the tiny buds that appeared on the ficus tree, the smallest beginnings are taking place, often just below the surface.

Some questions to consider in a season of waiting:

1. Different seasons of waiting call us to different responses. Like Simeon and Anna, perhaps you are being called to wait quietly, with expectant hope. Or maybe, like the Israelites exiled in Babylon, you are being called to settle in and get to work exactly where God has planted you right now. Or perhaps you are being called simply to watch, attentive, for God's presence in your life. If you are in a season of waiting, do you sense God calling you to wait in one of these particular ways? What does that look like for you?

2. "Attentiveness is vital to waiting," Sue Monk Kidd says. Write down one or two ways you could be more actively attentive, even in your small, daily moments of waiting. As I mentioned earlier, I most often experience God's presence in nature. Is there a particular place that more readily opens you to the experience of God's presence? Where is it? Can you go to that place regularly? Or even occasionally?

3. God addressed Jesus as "my beloved Son, in whom I am well pleased" (Matt. 3:17 KJV). Do you think of yourself in the same way, as God's beloved child, with whom he is well pleased? Why or why not?

4. When Jesus cried out to God in the Garden of Gethsemane on the night before his crucifixion, he used the intimate term for Father, "Abba," which is often translated as "Daddy." Try addressing God as "Abba" in prayer. Does using a more intimate name for God change how you perceive your relationship with him in any way? If so, how?

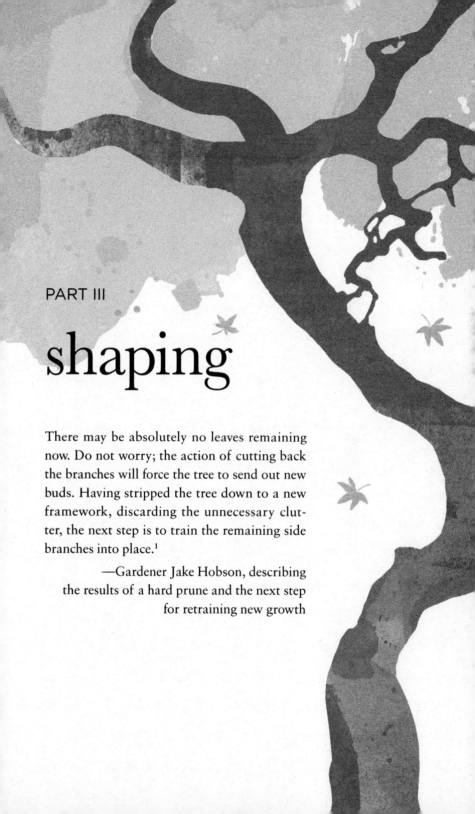

PART III

# shaping

There may be absolutely no leaves remaining now. Do not worry; the action of cutting back the branches will force the tree to send out new buds. Having stripped the tree down to a new framework, discarding the unnecessary clutter, the next step is to train the remaining side branches into place.[1]

—Gardener Jake Hobson, describing the results of a hard prune and the next step for retraining new growth

# 8

# twine and splint

## Two steps forward, one step back

> The needed change within us is God's work, not
> ours. The demand is for an inside job, and only
> God can work from the inside.
>
> —Richard Foster, *Celebration of Discipline*

Every spring, the tree in the corner of my backyard sprouts
dozens of seedlings at the bottom of its trunk. Sometimes
known as volunteers, adventitious buds, or my favorite sci-
entific term, *suckers*, these offspring grow not from seed, but
from tissue in the roots at the base or even some distance
from the tree. Around the middle of May each year, I hand
one of my kids a pair of garden clippers and send him out
to cut the shoots down to the ground, not only because the
masses of leaves and stems clumped around the trunk are

unsightly, but also because suckers are unhealthy for a tree, diverting nutrients and energy away from the crown.

After the errant suckers have been clipped to the ground, the back corner of my yard looks pristine and manicured, and I am pleased. But it never fails. A month or so after the pruning, a new crop of suckers has already begun to poke through the woodchips. After two months, they have all but obscured the base of the trunk again, and it's time to repeat the pruning.

Like the tree in my backyard, we, too, need to prune and prune again, especially when it comes to our own metaphorical "suckers." The branches we cut because we deem them unnecessary or even detrimental to our spiritual growth will often sprout again, sometimes even more vigorously than before. We become frustrated and discouraged when we realize that the progress we thought we made isn't necessarily permanent. We are humbled, knowing the journey toward uncovering our true selves is often a halting, stutter-step process. Sometimes it feels like we are walking two steps forward, one step back. Sometimes it feels more like two steps forward, three steps back.

The ancient Israelites were more than a little familiar with this cycle of spiritual progression and regression. Throughout their forty-year journey in the wilderness they wrestled with idolatry. Their idols were their most persistent branches, the "suckers" that, when cut from their lives, only cropped up again and again. The most obvious example of the Israelites' struggle with idolatry comes from Exodus 32, when, impatient with Moses' slow return from the mountaintop where he was convening with God, they begged second-in-command Aaron to make new gods to worship. Aaron was all too quick to comply, fashioning an idol in the shape of a golden calf from the earrings the Israelites handed over to him.

The golden calf may be the most infamous instance of idolatry in the Old Testament, but it's far from the only one. Even after the Israelites crossed the Jordan River and entered into the Promised Land, and even after the Lord ensured their victory over Jericho, they still fell prey to idolatry. Despite the fact that God had warned them not to hoard the gold, silver, bronze, and iron plundered from Jericho for themselves, one man couldn't help himself. Achan swiped a beautiful robe, 200 silver coins, and a bar of gold and, instead of dedicating the riches to God's treasury as the Lord had commanded, he buried them beneath his own tent.

Meanwhile, Joshua was mystified as to why God suddenly appeared to have turned against the Israelites. Soundly defeated in a battle they expected to win, Joshua cried out to God, "Oh, Sovereign Lord, why did you bring us across the Jordan River if you are going to let the Amorites kill us?" (Josh. 7:7 NLT).

It was only then that the leader learned his people had fallen prey to the lures of idolatry once again. The Israelites "have taken some of the devoted things; they have stolen, they have lied, they have put them with their own possessions" (v. 11) God explained to Joshua. That is why the Israelites have been defeated and why they have lost courage, God continues. "They turn their backs and run because they have been made liable to destruction" (v. 12).

*They have been made liable to destruction.* We need to pay attention to this, because identifying that which makes us liable to destruction is a critical part of the journey toward uncovering our true selves. As we still our bodies and minds, look hard at our false selves and our deepest desires, and continue to prune to an open center, we begin to see more clearly the idols and temptations that tax our souls, prevent us from living most fully and completely into our true selves, and draw us away from intimate relationship with God. This is a good time to ask ourselves some hard questions: What habits distract me and distance me from God? What weakens me and diminishes my trust in him? What fears cause me to lose courage, to falter, to flee?

For the Israelites—particularly Achan in this story—greed and a desire for power and control made them liable to destruction. And beneath their greed and desire for power and control was distrust. Achan distrusted God. He piled up treasures for himself because he did not trust in God's protection. Achan lived out of scarcity, rather than out of abundance. He tried to assure his own livelihood and future because he didn't trust that God would provide for him. His desire for power and control and his lack of trust in God made Achan liable to destruction, and his idolatry in turn made his fellow Israelites liable to destruction as well. Our sins can destroy not only ourselves but those around us.

An idol is anything that takes the place of God in our lives. This means idols can take an infinite variety of forms, from material wants like that gorgeous brick Tudor with the sprawling lawn and in-ground pool that just went up for sale three streets over, to more intangible desires like status, recognition, success, achievement, fame, control, or approval. A job can become an idol. Food, alcohol, or drugs can become idols. A relationship can become an idol. Timothy Keller says, "An idol is whatever you look at and say, in your heart of hearts, 'If I have that, then I'll feel my life has meaning, then I'll know I have value, then I'll feel significant and secure.'"[1] We have high expectations of our idols.

Idolatry is also insidious. An idol can weave its tendrils so subtly into your life, you may not even recognize it for what it is. For instance, my idolatry of success and achievement often masquerades as motivation, productivity, and the pursuit of excellence. This is not to say that motivation, productivity, or even a desire to achieve always signal a problem with idolatry, but simply that awareness of our own red flags can help us identify idolatry before it gets a stranglehold on our lives. When I look hard at my relentless productivity and busyness, I see they are actually by-products of a deeper desire to be successful, recognized, known, and, above all, loved.

Often more easily recognizable than the idols themselves, the by-products of our idols are the first clues that the branches we thought we pruned for good have sprouted again. Let me give you an example. I recently had dinner with two successful writer friends. Both are published authors. Both have substantial platforms and are well connected with some of the movers and shakers in the Christian publishing industry. I enjoyed chatting with them over cheesecake, but later, as I lay in bed replaying bits and pieces of the evening's conversation in my head, I felt a familiar sinking sensation yawn open in the pit of my stomach.

Suddenly I thought of a line from an Emily Dickinson poem: "I'm nobody! Who are you? Are you nobody, too?"[2] and I found myself chanting it over and over, mocking myself for my self-perceived inadequacies. It was, in short, a full-on pity party going on in my bed. When I thought about my friends' platforms, connections, and achievements, I felt very small in comparison. Very inconsequential. Very nobodyish.

And very envious.

Envy and jealousy are by-products of my idolatry. These feelings are like neon signs flashing "Danger! Danger!" When envy and jealousy clench at my gut, I know I'm getting too cozy with the idols of success, achievement, and the desire to be known. When I start to keep a scoreboard in my head of another author's Amazon rank or caliber of speaking gigs or number of readers or who she got to endorse her book, and I subsequently begin to feel envious or jealous because I don't measure up, I know it's time to take a hard look at my heart. As unpleasant as it is to come face-to-face with envy, jealousy, and other negative emotions, the silver lining is that the ugly offspring of idolatry can help us see when we need to retrieve the pruning shears, strip back the insidious, persistent suckers, and re-center ourselves in Christ once again.

Hustle, busyness, distraction, and anxiety are also by-products of my idolatry. When I find myself saying "yes" to every professional invitation to speak or write, filling my calendar with events, activities, and obligations, and running myself ragged with a mile-long to-do list, I know it's time to take a deep breath and a step back. Hustle mode is a red flag, a sign I need to take some time in solitude and quiet, to look hard at my priorities, and to ask myself what I am trying to achieve with all my self-important busyness.

Even the ways in which I use social media can signal that I am veering dangerously close to idolatry. "In proportion as our inward life fails, we go more constantly and desperately to the post-office," observed Henry David Thoreau in *Life without Principle.* "You may depend on it, that the poor fellow who walks away with the greatest number of letters, proud of his extensive correspondence, has not heard from himself this long while."[3]

Thoreau wrote those words nearly 200 years ago, but his observation is still relevant today. In other words, do we find ourselves constantly turning outward to seek affirmation and approval from others? Thoreau was talking about written correspondence, but social media makes this temptation that much easier for us in the twenty-first century. Constantly scrolling social media can be a sign that I am desperately seeking affirmation from my peers. When I find myself counting likes on a post or followers on a page, basing my sense of self-worth on social media engagement, or, even worse, monitoring how many likes my peers' posts have received and comparing myself to them, I know my social media use has veered from the realm of pleasure and entertainment into a habit that is making me liable to destruction.

It's not fun to look honestly at our weaknesses and flaws. It can be demoralizing and frustrating to identify our idols and temptations, to root out that which makes us liable to destruction. But it's also some of the most important work we will do on this journey toward wholeness. Naming our weaknesses, flaws, failures, and inabilities and calling out our idols ultimately creates space for us to move closer to Christ.

## Patience and Perseverance

So here's the question: Once we are able to identify and recognize the by-products of our idolatry, as well as the idols themselves, how do we begin to dismantle that which makes us liable to destruction? While the entire responsibility of transformation doesn't fall on our shoulders, we do have an important part to play in our journey toward wholeness. We participate in what God is doing in us and through us. As Richard Rohr says, the true self "is a house built on rock (Matt. 7:25), which does not mean it does not need constant maintenance, cleaning, and refinishing. The True Self is not the perfect self. It merely participates in the One who is."[4] So how do we participate in the transformative work God is doing in us? How do we keep the soul- and spirit-draining suckers—the shoots and branches that divert vital nutrients and which we have already pruned away—from sprouting again and again?

I wish I could say there is a quick and easy solution. Alas, there is not. Once again, we take our cue from the gardener.

Gardening expert Lee Reich, author of *The Pruning Book*, notes that the only effective way to eliminate suckers and reduce their opportunism is to stay vigilant and be persistent. "Keep on suckering," Reich advises. "Every year, even two to three times a year," cut back the shoots that sprout at the base of the tree.[5] If you are patient and persevere, eventually the tree will produce fewer and fewer suckers each year until finally, the root tissue at the base of the trunk will scar over and stop producing new shoots altogether.

Let's be honest; this is not the solution we want to hear, right? We want the quick fix, the magic formula. But in spiritual transformation, as in gardening, there is no fast and easy remedy. There is only patience, perseverance, and faith in the process. We participate in the pruning—we bring our weaknesses, failures, and flaws into the presence of Christ—and we put measures in place that will both loosen the idol's grasp on our lives and support our spiritual growth.

Let me give you an example from my own life. As I mentioned, I've identified social media, particularly Facebook, as something that, when I let it get out of hand, has the potential to make me liable to destruction. Social media fuels my idols—it makes me more likely to compare myself with my peers and to seek approval and affirmation from others. The bright lights of social media often blind me to my primary identity as a beloved child of God.

As a writer, connecting with readers online is something I enjoy, and it's an important part of my platform and book marketing. At the same time, it's also easy to let social media get the best of me, so I've had to take measures to keep the negative impact to a minimum. For example, last fall I deleted my Facebook app from my smartphone, so I don't have access to Facebook when I am away from my laptop. And last winter, as I mentioned earlier, I fasted from all social media for six weeks during Lent (which proved to be much more challenging than I had anticipated). I also try to limit my social media use on the weekends, especially on Sundays. These steps may sound simple, even a bit silly, but they've worked. Slowly, over time, I have decreased my dependence on social media and the time I spend there, and as a result, I am much less likely to suffer from its negative effects on my life.

> We participate in the pruning—we bring our weaknesses, failures, and flaws into the presence of Christ—and we put measures in place that will both loosen the idol's grasp on our lives and support our spiritual growth.

As my friend Lynn so wisely observed, "We tend to leave opportunities in our lives to be tempted by our idols." For a long time alcohol was a big idol for Lynn. "I had to take concrete steps to renounce it," she says, which included disposing of all the alcohol in her house, attending AA meetings for a while, not frequenting bars, and seeking God's help through prayer-journaling. Lynn put measures in place that not only reduced opportunities for the branch she cut to grow back, but also encouraged her remaining branches—her God-given gifts—to grow in the direction God was leading.

Telling a friend or loved one about your particular struggle with idolatry can help make you less liable to destruction as well. Ask someone to hold you accountable. For example, last year at my church's Ash Wednesday service, we were invited to write the sin we were struggling with on a small slip of paper. The papers were collected and contained in vases on the altar until Easter Sunday, when they were burned in a bonfire during the sunrise service. Last year I wrote "my addiction to social media" on the slip of paper. Although it was a private exchange between God and me, simply naming the sin and knowing my paper was among those in the vase on the altar held me accountable. I also announced my social media fast publicly on Facebook and Instagram the day before I started, and I told my husband and kids about the fast. I knew I would be less likely to peek at my accounts if there was a risk of getting caught.

Idolatry is insidious. Like the persistent suckers at the base of a tree, our idols can be relentless. Just when we think we've rid ourselves of them for good, they sprout again, which is why it's so important to think carefully about the practices and habits that can help inhibit regrowth, as well as the people in our lives who can support and encourage us along the way.

## New Directions

Gardener Jake Hobson notes that once a tree is stripped down to its basic framework with the "unnecessary clutter" discarded, "the next step is to train the remaining side branches into place."[6] The gardener ties the branches that are left with twine or parcel string in the direction he or she wants them to grow. Some branches, Hobson notes, will be more flexible than others, and flexibility can be affected by the season (branches are suppler during the spring and summer, when sap is flowing through the plant). Thicker branches may need to be splinted in order to redirect their growth, and some branches, says Hobson, may be too thick and rigid to train at all. The solution in these cases is to cut the branch and retrain the resulting growth instead.

The metaphor is a rich one when we apply it to our spiritual lives. Think, for example, about the role of the twine and the splint in retraining tree branches to grow in a particular direction. In other words, what practices or spiritual disciplines can we put in place that will both support our spiritual growth and curb our tendencies toward idolatry?

When we hear the term *spiritual discipline*, we often think of ancient rituals like fasting, honoring the Sabbath, the Benedictine practice of *lectio divina*, or the Ignatian practice of the daily *examen*. I have explored many of these disciplines and found them to be spiritually fruitful, but I'd also argue that even an ordinary chore or routine can be transformed into an unconventional spiritual discipline of sorts. At different points in my life, running, weeding, painting walls and trim, and walking the dog have all served as rich spiritual practices that have helped draw me closer to God. These disciplines, even when they don't look "spiritual" on the outside, can serve as the twine and the splint, supporting us and helping us to retrain our remaining healthy branches in the direction God is leading us. "By themselves, spiritual disciplines can do nothing; they can only get us to the place where something can be done," says Richard Foster. "They are God's means of grace . . . the means by which we place ourselves where he can bless us."[7]

One of my favorite unconventional spiritual disciplines is what the Japanese call *shinrin-yoku*, or "forest bathing" (although, since I live in Nebraska, it might more accurately be called "prairie bathing")—the practice of spending time in the forest or in nature generally. *Shinrin-yoku* was first developed in Japan during the 1980s and has become an important part of preventive health care and healing in Japanese medicine.[8] Apparently the Japanese have known for quite some time what Western scientists are only beginning to substantiate now, which is the fact that spending time in nature is good for us. It lowers our blood pressure and reduces cortisol levels. It increases the cancer-fighting white blood cells and allows the prefrontal cortex part of our brains to rest, which kicks in the brain's default mode network.

Remember when we talked about the importance of directed rest in chapter 1? As it turns out, spending time in nature—even as little as twenty-five minutes in a city park or green space[9]—encourages our brains to enter into a state of directed rest, which is good not only for our cognitive functioning and creativity, but also for our souls. The activation of the default mode network "is what enables us to imagine other perspectives and scenarios, imagine the future, remember the past, understand ourselves and others, and create meaning from our experiences," observes science journalist Carolyn Gregoire.[10] In other words, we are able to see our true selves and our reasons for being more clearly when we are in a state of directed rest.

Of course, spiritual disciplines—the metaphorical twine and splint that support the branches we want to grow—are effective only to the degree we use them. Being in nature is one of the primary ways in which I connect with God and where I most often sense his presence, yet taking time to get outdoors, notice my surroundings, and appreciate the uniqueness and beauty of God's creation is one of the first things I neglect when I let busyness get the best of me. It's easy for me to forget all about the importance of a stroll around the lake or five minutes on a park bench when I insist on spinning as fast as the world demands.

Just recently I was reminded of the importance of *shinrin-yoku* in my life, and what happens when I neglect it. It was a Monday evening—time for soccer practice and my night to drive the carpool. I pulled up to the curb in front of Dakota and Cole's house—Rowan's friends and soccer teammates—and lightly tapped my horn. Seeing no movement inside, I told Rowan to run up the front walk and knock on the front door to retrieve his friends.

"No one's answering!" he called down to me, shrugging.

"Knock again, louder this time," I yelled out the passenger window over the steady hum of the car engine. My hands tightened on the steering wheel, and I felt my pulse begin to quicken. We were going to be late, and I hate being late for anything, even something as unimportant as a YMCA youth league soccer practice.

Rowan knocked again. Still no answer. I motioned him back to the car, but just as he was pulling on his seat belt, I saw the front door swing open. Dakota and Cole's mom stepped onto the porch and leaned over the railing. "What's going on? Are you here to pick up the boys? It's my night . . . I was just leaving!" she called down, clearly puzzled.

She was right. Monday is her night to drive the three boys to soccer practice. For the past two months she's driven Monday nights and I've driven Thursdays, and yet there I was, sitting frantic and flummoxed outside her house on the wrong night.

The soccer carpool mix-up was a wake-up call to bench myself. Literally. I hadn't realized until that moment that I'd been neglecting my daily practice of bench-sitting and forest bathing. I have a lot on my plate these days—book writing, speaking engagements, a part-time job, shuttling kids to an endless lineup of soccer games and cross country meets and tennis practice, and squeezing housework and errands in wherever I can. Focused on simply getting through my myriad responsibilities each day, it had been more than two weeks since I'd settled into five minutes of quiet on my far side of the wilderness. As the boys piled into the backseat and I sped off toward soccer practice, I knew I needed to still myself, even as the world continued to spin around me.

The very next evening I was back at my bench by the path. As I sat, I watched two goldfinches feast on coneflower in the ravine, yellow feathers flashing amid swaying stalks. A red-bellied woodpecker tapped a staccato beat, bobbing up a nearby tree trunk, pausing every few inches to prod at the bark. I noticed the leaves of the ginkgo tree were just beginning to turn. In a few weeks the grass would be carpeted in gold.

I remember who I am in this quiet place on the far side of the wilderness. I hear God's voice here, in the wind lifting the leaves, in the tap of a woodpecker's beak on bark. I feel God's touch here, in the sun, warm on my hair; in the breeze, gentle on my face. This quiet, this stillness, this green and gold, these are God's love letters to me. "Only in returning to me and resting in me will you be saved," the Holy One reminds me (Isa. 30:15 NLT). I return to this bench and I rest, remembering that I am blessed and beloved.

## Trust in the Slow Work of God

If you're a "make it happen" kind of person like me, you may forget from time to time that the responsibility for spiritual transformation isn't all yours. In all your pruning and shaping and retraining and disciplining, you could begin to think that transformation is all up to you. Let me remind you: it's not. God does the work of transformation in us; we show up and try to provide the circumstances in which God can best do his work.

After I returned from my trip to Italy, I worried that what God had begun in me under the Tuscan sun would not continue in my everyday, ordinary life in Nebraska. I worried that the invitation into relationship and intimacy I'd received and begun to answer in Italy would be lost bit by bit amid laundry, to-do lists, deadlines, and dentist appointments, until nothing but a faint memory, like a fogged image in an antique mirror, remained. I didn't trust my ability to keep the spark lit that God had ignited in my heart. More importantly, I wasn't convinced God would continue to fan that spark into an enduring flame.

Less than three weeks after I returned to Nebraska, I was back on a plane, this time flying with my family to New England to celebrate my parents' fiftieth anniversary. I'd brought my Bible, and during the flight, I read these words from Philippians, a verse I'd read numerous times before: "And I am certain that God, who began the good work within you, will continue his work until it is finally finished on the day when Christ Jesus returns" (Phil. 1:6 NLT).

In the past, I'd always understood these words as a promise related to my vocation as a writer. I interpreted the verse to mean that since God had given me the gift of and the passion for writing, he would nurture that gift and ensure a fruitful harvest (i.e., successful books). To me this was a verse about outcomes. I see now, though, that this is a myopic understanding of Paul's words. The truth is, God's plans and his vision are always far bigger than we can possibly imagine. When I read Paul's words to the Philippians as we winged our way from Nebraska to New England, I understood this "good work" was much more than my next book or my success as a writer. Paul reminded me that God is in the business of transformation and relationship.

God himself extends the invitation into intimacy. God himself ignites the spark in our hearts and keeps the flame burning. And God himself, who begins the good work in us, will continue his work from now until the end of our time on earth. We needn't clutch tight-fisted in fear, anxious that what has been started will evaporate like mist off a pond's surface on a cool autumn morning. God is in control of this process. He is the Inviter. He is the Igniter. And he can be trusted not only to continue but to complete what he begins.

That day on the airplane I remembered a moment that had taken place many months earlier, long before my trip to Italy. One night, on the edge of sleep, I heard seven words reverberate in my head, clear as day, almost as if they had been uttered out loud. I hadn't been praying. As far as I can remember, I hadn't even been thinking about anything in particular. Yet suddenly, out of nowhere, I heard a proclamation: "I have so much more for you." That was it—a seven-word declaration that appeared to drop from the sky. Somehow I knew it wasn't one of my own thoughts that had bubbled up from my subconscious to the surface. Somehow I knew it was God.

> God is in control of this process. He is the Inviter. He is the Igniter. And he can be trusted not only to continue but to complete what he begins.

I wrote those seven words into my journal the next morning, but it wasn't until I read Paul's declaration to the Philippians many months later that I understood their true meaning. God does indeed have so much more for us than we could ever possibly imagine, and what he has for us is not always what we think it will be or even what we think we want. Our vision is limited. We tend to hold on to the wrong things—wealth, ambition, acclaim, outcomes. But God? He's holding on to only one thing. God is holding tightly to you and me, and no matter what, he won't let go. The "so much more" God promised me wasn't related to book sales or achievement or success. It was much better and much bigger than all that. The "so much more" was more of God himself—the deepest desire I didn't even know I had.

We will not be made wholly and completely perfect, we will not be wholly and completely transformed, until Christ returns. Only then, when he reconciles heaven and earth, when the kingdom comes (see Rev. 21:1–5), will everything be set beautifully and perfectly right once and for all. God begins his good work in each one of us. He continues that good work with our participation each and every day of our lives here on earth. And he will finish that good work when he makes not only us but all things new.

"Trust in the slow work of God," wrote Jesuit priest Pierre Teilhard de Chardin. "Only God could say what this new spirit gradually forming within you will be. Give our Lord the benefit of believing that his hand is leading you. And accept the anxiety of feeling yourself in suspense and incomplete."[11] There is anxiety in incompleteness to be sure. But there is also peace in the relinquishing, in knowing that God continues his good work in us and through us, even when we can't yet see what will be.

## GOING DEEPER

In spiritual transformation, as in gardening, there are seasons of rapid growth and development, seasons of dormancy, and even seasons in which it looks like regression, rather than progression, is taking place. Do not despair; God is working in you and through you, even when you cannot discern his presence. Try, as Pierre Teilhard de Chardin urged, "to accept the anxiety of feeling yourself . . . incomplete."

Here are some questions to consider as you walk stutter-step toward wholeness:

1. Can you identify the "suckers" in your life—the un-wanted branches or stems that reappear again and again, even after you have tried to prune them?

2. Can you think of any bad habits or persistent idols that make you liable to destruction? Can you identify the by-products of these idols—the sins that alert you to an idol that has a stranglehold on you?

3. What splints and twine—traditional or unconventional disciplines—could you put in place to help support your spiritual growth and diminish your tendency toward idolatry?

4. Are you able to identify or name the good work that God has begun in you? If so, take a moment to offer thanks to the God who cherishes you and who will see it through to completion. If you are not able to identify the good work God is doing in your life right now, are you able to believe that he is doing a work you can't yet discern?

# 9

## way opens

### On coming alive

When you get your "Who am I?" question right,
all the "What should I do?" questions tend to take
care of themselves.

—Richard Rohr, *Falling Upward*

Growing up, I was surrounded by teachers. My dad was
a middle school special education teacher, and then later
a high school guidance counselor. My best friend's dad
was a middle school math teacher. My soccer coach was
a teacher. Many of my parents' friends and the parents of
my peers were teachers. I assumed I would be a teacher
too. I had always loved to read. I was a decent writer. My
favorite subject was English. It was a no-brainer: I should
be a high school English teacher.

My dad encouraged me in this direction. Teaching is a good, stable job, especially for a woman, he said. "You'll have your summers off," he reminded me. "It will be ideal when you have kids." These sounded like logical reasons to pursue a career as a teacher. When I was accepted at the state university, I double-majored in English and Secondary Education. I completed all the required courses, did my semester of student teaching at my former high school, and passed the state certification exam. It wasn't until I began interviewing for high school teaching positions that I realized I had made a grave mistake. Turns out, I didn't want to be a high school English teacher. The truth is, I never had.

There had been hints along the way—like the fact that I'd found my education classes frightfully boring and had hated almost every moment of my four months in the classroom as a student teacher. I enjoyed prepping my classes, grading papers, and brainstorming creative ways to introduce challenging material to my students, but I despised the actual teaching. It wasn't only that I was a little bit afraid of my students (though that was certainly part of it; my legs trembled and my hands shook every time I stood in front of the classroom). I also somehow knew, almost immediately, that teaching wasn't the right fit for me.

Still, I pressed on. Secondary teaching certificate in hand, I applied to several high school English teacher jobs across the state. Like a train chugging dutifully down the track, I never considered not applying. Teaching was the path I had chosen, and getting a job as a high school English teacher was the expected culmination of my four-year degree. There was no switching tracks now.

My saving grace was that I was not offered any of the teaching positions I applied to. I came close—I had several interviews, and even a few callbacks—but in the end, the jobs were offered to other applicants. Though I was terrified by the fact that I had no job and no direction, I was secretly relieved. I had no idea what I would do with an English degree, but I knew one thing for sure: I was glad, come September, I would not be standing in a high school classroom.

You may wonder how in the world I came so close to embarking upon a career path so unsuitable for me. But according to author and teacher Parker Palmer, my story is not unusual. "We arrive in this world with birthright gifts— then we spend the first half of our lives abandoning them or letting others disabuse us of them," Palmer explains in his book *Let Your Life Speak*.[1]

My dad didn't disabuse me of my gifts—he recognized my skills as a communicator, my rapport with others, and my energetic personality, and he knew these assets were a good match for a career in teaching. Having flourished for decades as an educator himself, he also understood the benefits and rewards of this particular career path, and, wanting me to experience the same satisfaction he had, he steered me in that direction. What he didn't and couldn't know was that while some of my natural gifts were a good match for teaching, I didn't have the heart for it. I was missing the passion. I followed my father's direction because I knew being a teacher would be a solid job, a respectable profession, and a safe choice. I pursued a career in teaching because I thought it was what I ought to do. Given my strengths, it made sense. But all along I was missing a critical component. Teaching didn't make me come alive.

## Proceed as the Way Opens

Every fall, loppers and pruning shears in hand, my husband and I plunge headlong into the thicket of spirea shrubs that grow along the inside of the picket fence in our backyard. Aptly named bridal veil spirea, the bushes are beautiful in May, when, laden with thousands of delicate white blossoms, the branches cascade lacy and lush like yards of gossamer tulle to the ground. Unfortunately, for the remaining eleven months of the year, the shrubs are unruly and brambly and not especially attractive, and so every fall, Brad and I attempt to tame the chaos.

After hours of cutting, shearing, and clipping, we emerge bloody and scratched from the shrubs and stand back to survey our work, and every year, without fail, the spirea inevitably looks worse than when we began. Not only are the shrubs still a brambly, chaotic mess, our pruning also typically results in large gaps in the foliage. Rather than a neatly manicured hedge like we envisioned, we are left with an unkempt mix of errant branches and twigs interspersed with gaping bald spots. We stand in the backyard, clipped branches littering the lawn at our feet, and shake our heads, convinced that we've ruined the spirea once and for all.

The funny thing is, in sixteen years of annual autumn pruning, we have yet to decimate the spirea. In fact, come spring, it's apparent that just the opposite has happened. The gaping holes and glaring empty spaces we created with our shears and loppers in the fall have miraculously been covered over with new shoots and blooms. What was once a void is now filled in with healthy new growth.

The Quakers have a saying: "Proceed as the way opens," which is a lot like my father's adage, "When in conflict, do nothing." To "proceed as the way opens" means to avoid taking hasty action and to wait for guidance or future circumstances to inform your decision.[2] As with the pruned spirea shrubs in my backyard, sometimes a space appears, allowing a new way to open and be filled. What initially might look like a mistake may in fact allow the space necessary for a new blooming.

Shortly after finishing my master's degree, I landed a job as an editor in New York City, first at a business magazine and then at an art publication. I loved magazine editing and was good at it, but, it turned out, I did not thrive in the city. The frenetic pace overwhelmed me, the constant noise and throngs of people crushed my spirit, and I deeply missed easy access to nature. After two years in Manhattan, I succumbed to a debilitating chronic illness that forced me to resign from my editor job and move back in with my parents in Massachusetts. It appeared at the time that my stint in New York City had been a mistake.

Later, after I had recovered from my illness, I accepted a job as a communications director at a community college, only to learn through trial and error that I am not particularly skilled at managing people. The day I burst into tears when a staff member quit because, as he put it, he couldn't bear working for me a minute longer, was the day I realized I rather disliked being a boss and was, frankly, not very good at it. Once again, it seemed like my career choice had been a mistake.

For a long time, my professional life looked a lot like the pruned spirea shrubs in my backyard. It was a tangled mess with lots of lopped off branches and glaring empty spaces. What I couldn't see at the time, however, was that my mistakes and wrong turns were actually making space for a new, clearer way to open and be filled.

Turns out, we can learn as much from our mistakes and limitations as we can from our successes and potential. While both experiences as a magazine editor in New York City and as a community college communications director were difficult and disappointing at the time, both, in highlighting my limitations, were instrumental in ultimately pointing me toward my potential. Those "failed" professional endeavors helped me learn that I am better suited to small-town rather than big-city living, and that I am happier self-employed or as a member of a staff rather than as a boss. Ultimately, the branches I pruned, though they created gaps in my professional life and certainly felt like failures at the time, opened the space to pursue my calling as a writer.

## How to Figure Out Who You Are

There is a difference between who we feel obligated to be, or who society or other influencers say we ought to be, and who we really are. "Figure out who you are. Then do it on purpose," advised Dolly Parton.[3] Or as Mark Twain put it: "The two best days of your life are the day you were born and the day you find out why."[4]

Long before Mark Twain and Dolly Parton, even the apostle Paul had something to say about this. "Make a careful exploration of who you are and the work you have been given, and then sink yourself into that," he wrote to the

Galatians. "Each of you must take responsibility for doing the creative best you can with your own life" (Gal. 6:4–5 Message). The question is, *How* do we figure out who we are? *How* do we figure out why we were born? What are the breadcrumbs that will lead us along the path to our calling when we are lost and can't find our way?

Parker Palmer suggests that one way to pick up the trail to our true self and calling is to look back to our youth, when we "lived closer to our birthright gifts."[5] I laughed when I first read that, remembering the day I stumbled upon my old diaries crammed into a cardboard box marked "Michelle's Keepsakes" in a corner of our basement. I sat on the concrete floor, cringing as I flipped through the pages. Suffice it to say, my fervent declarations of love both for boys and pop music ("Mr. Roboto is my favorite song!" is written in giant puffy rainbow letters across one entire page of my diary) are not exactly prescient signs of my future calling as a writer.

Still, when I recall my childhood passions, I do see hints of the vocational calling that would emerge decades later. For instance, my greatest pleasure as a child and preteen was reading. Tucked into the crook of an apple tree in my backyard, I lost myself in mysteries and adventures, particularly those that featured strong female protagonists—Nancy Drew, *Mrs. Frisby and the Rats of NIHM*, *The Secret Garden*, *Island of the Blue Dolphins*, Pippi Longstocking, and everything by Judy Blume. I also loved biography, especially stories about girls or women who forged new paths or overcame great obstacles—Florence Nightingale, Clara Barton, Helen Keller, Anne Frank. I could get lost for hours amid the stacks in my town library, and later, in middle school and high school, I delighted in the in-depth research required for history and English papers. The clues are subtle, but they are there. Hidden in my zeal for reading and research were hints of the books I would write decades later.

Our birthright gifts are also often those we are least able to recognize in ourselves. For years I lamented the fact that I didn't have any talents. I yearned to play piano, sing soprano, or paint oil portraits. I viewed musicians and artists as people with true gifts, while I considered my own writing ability a useful but pedestrian skill. It never occurred to me that my skills as a writer were a gift. I took it for granted, all the while pining for a "real" talent. Before I began to write books, people would often ask me, when they discovered I had majored in English, if I ever wrote fiction or poetry. "Oh no, I'm not creative; I'm just a business writer," I always answered. *Just* a business writer. I didn't value my skills. I couldn't see that the ability to craft accessible, readable prose is itself a gift.

Turns out, Paul's suggestion to "make a careful exploration of who you are and the work you have been given" is sound advice. Looking back at what kinds of activities energized us and brought us joy as children and young adults can offer useful insights into our God-given gifts. Likewise, looking at what we are naturally good at, especially those skills we overlook or take for granted, might offer a path toward uncovering our vocational sweet spot.

### Our Lives Are a Listening

In early Christianity, the word *vocation* originally referred to the call by God of an individual to the religious life. Even today, when we hear the word *vocation*, we may first think of a pastor, a priest, a nun, or a missionary, but the truth is, a vocation is much more than a religious calling. Each of us is called by God, and as Paul reminded the Romans, "God's gifts and his call are irrevocable" (Rom. 11:29). The word *vocation* comes from the Latin *vox*, meaning "voice," and *vocare*, which means "to call." The whole notion of a calling depends on there being a Caller. The Caller calls, and we answer, but first we listen. As Thomas Merton wrote, "My life is a listening; His is a speaking."[6]

Sometimes, though, we don't recognize God's voice; we can't discern that he is, in fact, speaking. Such was the case with young Samuel in the Old Testament.

Samuel was dedicated to God by his mother, Hannah, as part of a vow she made before he was born (see 1 Sam. 1:24–28). After he was weaned, Samuel went to live in the temple to serve Eli, the high priest. Each night Samuel slept in the tabernacle, where the ark of God was kept. One night, God called Samuel, but Samuel, thinking it was Eli who had called him, ran to his master and said, "Here I am; you called me" (1 Sam. 3:5). Confused, Eli sent Samuel back to bed. Three times the Lord called Samuel, and three times Samuel leapt from bed and ran to Eli's side (see vv. 5, 6, 8).

Finally, as Samuel stood by his bedside for the third time, Eli realized it was God who was calling his young servant. "Go and lie down," Eli instructed Samuel, "and if he calls you, say, 'Speak, LORD, for your servant is listening'" (v. 9). The fourth and final time Samuel heard his name being called into the darkness, he recognized the voice as God's and responded as Eli had instructed. Samuel then received his first assignment from God in his role as God's prophet, which was to convey a difficult message to Eli about his sons (see vv. 11–14).

A few months after my second book released, my editor, Chad, and I were chatting one morning on the phone, brainstorming ideas for another book. "If you could write a full-length biography about any of the fifty women featured in your last book, who would you choose?" he asked me. I didn't hesitate. "Katharina Luther," I answered. The wife of Protestant reformer Martin Luther captivated me. The basic research I had done to write a short chapter about her in my previous book had left me eager to know more.

Chad was thrilled. I could hear the excitement building in his voice as we talked. With the 500th anniversary of the Protestant Reformation around the corner, 2017 was the perfect time to publish a new biography of the Luthers, he reasoned. I, on the other hand, was already regretting I'd suggested the idea. The problem was, when I considered the dozens, if not hundreds of books that had already been published about Martin Luther over the years, I felt underqualified and just plain not smart enough to add to the oeuvre. I imagined an academic writing a book about Katharina and Martin Luther—someone who smoked a pipe, listened to opera on NPR, and was able to read German.

Instead of writing a proposal for the book, as Chad had suggested, I did nothing. I didn't pursue the idea; I didn't even seriously consider it. Until, that is, I happened to mention the idea in a conversation with three close friends, all of whom insisted not only that I was qualified to write this book, but also that perhaps God was calling me to do so.

I hadn't seen it that way at all. Like Samuel, I hadn't recognized God's voice, and like Samuel, I needed an Eli in my life to point me in the direction of God's calling. The truth is, my own ideas and expectations of who I was as a writer had blinded me to the opportunity looking me square in the face. I didn't hear the call because it didn't sound exactly the way I'd imagined and expected it should. Turns out, I had been listening to my own voice—the voice of fear and insecurity—rather than listening to God's.

It's not easy to identify the voice of God. Myriad distractions vie for our attention—not the least of which is our own ego (in my case, that's often the loudest voice of all). We all need an Eli to help us sort through the detritus. We all need an Eli to help us discern when God is calling, especially if we can't hear his voice ourselves.

### Living from the Inside Out

On one of our free afternoons in Italy, a half dozen or so of the writers attending the retreat convened a meeting to brainstorm and share strategies and ideas related to book marketing.

Initially I was excited. Several of these authors have a much bigger audience and platform than I have, and I was eager to gain insight into their success. I took copious notes in my journal as they chatted about utilizing social media, creating and launching online classes, and strategies for growing email subscriber lists. While I listened, I made a list of the steps I needed to take in order to put several of these new ideas in place.

About halfway through the meeting, though, I realized that dread and anxiety had overtaken my initial enthusiasm.

The writers who were sharing about their successful business strategies were energized—clearly they enjoyed the entrepreneurial side of creative work—but I was not, and it took me a while to figure out why.

As the writers continued to chat, I thought about the fact that I am not an early adopter. Ever. I considered that I don't like to experiment with new technologies, and that I am easily overwhelmed when faced with a new initiative. I also admitted to myself that I don't relish the challenge of figuring out innovative strategies and how they might work for me. In short, I realized the reason I was filled with dread and anxiety is that while I am a writer and an author, I do not have an entrepreneurial spirit. It took me a while to remember that this is okay.

One of the reasons we struggle so much with the process of discovering our vocational sweet spot is that we often force ourselves to be someone we are not. We try to squeeze our square peg selves into a round hole. The problem, though, is that when the person we are striving to be doesn't jibe with our true, authentic self, we wind up feeling frustrated and fragmented in our work. Sometimes we even end up doing work that fills us with dread and anxiety instead of work that makes us come alive. That afternoon at the writers' gathering, I forgot who I was. I am not an entrepreneur, yet when I made a list of all the entrepreneurial things I was going to do to become "a successful author," I tried, at least for a few minutes, to will myself to be one. I took what I was hearing on the outside and tried to make myself that on the inside.

It's said that Michelangelo intentionally left some of his sculptures incomplete to represent man's eternal struggle to free himself from the trappings of the world. Visitors to the Accademia Gallery in Florence can view some of these unfinished sculptures along the corridor leading to Michelangelo's *David*, which looms massive in the center of the main gallery. During my trip to Italy I stood speechless in front of each of these unfinished sculptures, known as the four *Prisoners*, or *Slaves*, as our docent explained Michelangelo's sculpting technique. Unlike most Renaissance sculptors, who prepared a plaster cast model and then marked the block of marble to know where to chisel and chip, Michelangelo mostly worked freehand, starting from the front of the block and working back. He believed the sculptor was a tool in God's hand, "not creating but simply revealing the powerful figures already contained in the marble."[7] Michelangelo insisted that the essential sculptural act was one of *levare*—taking away, a subtractive process[8]—much like the role of the gardener with pruning shears in hand.

This process of taking away to reveal what's already inside resonates with me when it comes to how I have begun to think about calling as well. As Meister Eckhart put it, "The soul does not grow by addition but by subtraction."[9] God created each of us with unique gifts and an essential, authentic self, but sometimes these gifts and this true self lay hidden, as if buried beneath a ton of marble. Like the sculptor who allows the art to emerge from inanimate material, or the gardener who prunes a tree to reveal its essential elements,

> Like the sculptor who allows the art to emerge from inanimate material, we, too, await God's direction and then follow his lead as he reveals our true gifts.

we, too, await God's direction and then follow his lead as he reveals our true gifts. We still ourselves. We wait with hope. We look and listen. And then, when the time is right, we walk toward the way that opens, toward the space that only we can fill.

## What Makes You Come Alive?

"Cultivating a wholehearted life is not like trying to reach a destination," writes Brené Brown. "It's like walking toward a star in the sky. We never really arrive, but we certainly know that we're heading in the right direction."[10] The truth is, figuring out who you are and the work you are called to—what Brown calls "cultivating a wholehearted life"—is a lifelong process. Like the bridal veil spirea in my backyard, living into your calling entails observation, tweaking, and even radical pruning all along the way. You may bloom for years in your vocational sweet spot, only to realize at some point that a way is closing or a new way is opening. Or you might backslide a bit, the quiet voice of the Holy Spirit diminished by the clamor of your false self or the distractions of the world. Yet if we continue to offer ourselves space and quiet, our true selves will offer us hints along the way, both when we are veering off course and when we're heading in the right direction.

Sometimes simply noticing how our body feels can offer insight into whether we are listening to and heeding our true self. For instance, I often get a pit in my stomach when I am heading down the wrong path, as if my body instinctively knows what's right or wrong, even before my mind does. Likewise, as we discussed in the previous chapter, it's important to be aware of that which makes us liable to destruction. When I feel envy, jealousy, or the urge to ramp up productivity, I can be pretty sure my idolatry of success, which is driven by my false self, has taken hold again.

On the other hand, we can also notice what enlivens, excites, or enriches us. What brings you joy? Contentment? Satisfaction? What makes you come alive? What gives you life? As the Olympic runner Eric Liddell said in the film *Chariots of Fire*, "I believe God made me for a purpose. But he also made me fast. When I run I feel His pleasure."[11] Is there something in which, when you are immersed in it, you feel God's pleasure? God gives us a purpose and a calling; he gives us work to do in our time on earth. But he also desires that we will experience satisfaction and even delight in our work, and when we do, I believe this gives God pleasure too.

A few months ago I spotted my former boss when I was out shopping with my son Noah in Marshall's. My initial instinct was to avoid him, not because I harbored any ill feelings, but simply because I hadn't seen him in a couple of years, and I thought a conversation in the menswear section might be awkward. I walked out the store's automatic sliding doors and into the parking lot, but before I made it to my car, I stopped short and turned to Noah. "We need to go back inside," I told him. "I have to say hi to my old boss."

Noah tried to convince me to leave. "It's fine," he argued. "He didn't even see you. Why do you need to talk to him?

Let's just go!" Honestly, I wasn't at all sure why I felt the need to return to the store and strike up a conversation with my former boss. Maybe it was intuition. Maybe it was guilt. But whatever the impetus, I turned around and headed back through the automatic doors to the men's section of Marshall's, Noah trailing grumpily behind me.

Jeff and I chatted for a few minutes over a rack of polo shirts. During our conversation I learned he was working for The Salvation Army headquarters in Omaha. "If you ever need a freelance writer, let me know," I suggested, handing Jeff my business card before we parted. Two months later, he hired me.

I've been writing part-time for The Salvation Army for almost two years now, and I love it. I've found my calling, "the place," as theologian Frederick Buechner said, "where [my] deep gladness and the world's hunger meet."[12] It's not glamorous work. An article I wrote recently about Stephen, a recovering meth addict who is one year clean and on the road back to physical and mental health, for example, was included in a newsletter that was mailed to fewer than 800 people, and I suspect far fewer than that actually read the story. This work won't impact book sales, help me build my platform, or earn me any name recognition. There's no status in this kind of writing. And yet, the day I interviewed him on the phone, the perseverance, strength, and humility I heard in Stephen's voice awoke something in me. Talking with Stephen and writing his story was some of the most gratifying work I've ever done because it's work that was born out of my authentic self, rather than out of hustle, striving, and the need to be Someone Important.

In a recent podcast interview, author Andy Crouch noted that when we focus solely on status—on being the biggest, the best, and the most successful—we lose the opportunity to use our gifts to benefit others rather than ourselves. "Everyone is chasing status," Crouch observed, "but serving the vulnerable is wide open in every field."[13] So often I find myself wildly spinning my wheels in a fruitless attempt to become Someone Important. Yet in doing so, I leave in my wake a vast expanse of potential to make a difference in a less conspicuous but no less important way. Setting our sights so narrowly on reaching whatever it is we've deemed The One Big Thing means we often miss the wide-open field of less glamorous but no less gratifying work available to us.

Discovering your true calling, the place your deep gladness meets the world's hunger, won't likely bring you status, accolades, or notoriety. It probably won't make you "successful" by our culture's standards. But this I know for sure: it will offer you the opportunity for a different but no less beautiful kind of greatness, the kind of greatness that will bring you satisfaction and contentment, the kind of greatness that will make you come alive and bless you unexpectedly beyond measure.

Many years ago I worked part-time as an obituary writer for my local city newspaper. It was my job to synthesize the milestones and highlights of the deceased person's life into a concise biography that, depending on the person, would fill as little as a paragraph or as much as a page. I wrote the obituaries of lots of different people, from those who had been CEOs, doctors, professors, and attorneys to those who had worked as auto mechanics, elementary school teachers, nurse's aides, and mail carriers.

I was reminded of that job recently as I listened to the late poet John O'Donohue talk about the difference between biography and identity in a podcast interview. "There's a reduction of identity to biography," O'Donohue observed, but "they're not the same thing. Biography unfolds identity and makes it visible and puts the mirror of it out there, but identity is a more complex thing. Your identity is not equivalent to your biography."[14]

> Your identity is not equivalent to your biography.

Your identity comes not from what you do, but from who you are in God. Once you understand at the core of your being that you are truly God's beloved—delighted in and cherished by God—everything else falls into place. Some of us may end up with a paragraph for our obituary, some of us with a page, but the truth is, it doesn't matter because our biography is not who we are. It is important and good to use our God-given gifts wisely in our short time on Earth, to be sure, but as Jesus gently reminded his friend Martha in the midst of all her frantic doing and serving, what we do—even the fabulous things we do—is not the most important thing (see Luke 10:38–42).

Above all, God wants to be in relationship with us. He isn't nearly as concerned with what we do as he is with who we are, and especially who we are in him. Our primary identity is Beloved, and our very name is written in the palm of his hand (see Isa. 49:16 NLT). In the same way God called his precious son Beloved, he names our identity. Listen to the quiet whisper in your soul. God calls you Beloved too.

## GOING DEEPER

Figuring out who you are and what you should do with your "one wild and precious life," as the poet Mary Oliver says, isn't easy.[15] We don't always recognize our God-given gifts. We don't always recognize the voice of God himself, even when he tells us to turn right or left, even when he says, "This is the way" (Isa. 30:21). May these questions help to shine a little light along the path as you journey toward answering the essential question "Who am I?"

1. Think back to your childhood. Can you identify any of what Parker Palmer calls your "birthright gifts"? What are they? If you've lost sight of your early passions, how could you begin to circle back to unearth those long-buried gifts?

2. Of everything you've done in your life, which achievement of yours do you feel best about? They needn't be "important"; think about what made you feel thoroughly satisfied.

3. Consider Paul's advice to "make a careful exploration of who you are and the work you have been given"

(Gal. 6:4 Message). How is your current work aligned or misaligned with your essential self?

4. Who in your life could be an Eli—someone who can help you hear God's voice and discern his calling for you?

5. What would it look like for you to pursue a greatness born out of satisfaction and a sense of true fulfillment rather than out of notoriety or success?

# 10

# water, wood, air, and stone

## We are better together

We are lost unless we can recover compassion. . . .
We must find, once more, community, a sense of
family, of belonging to each other.

—Madeleine L'Engle, *Circle of Quiet*

I still cringe when I remember how I sobbed that morning, squeezed against the sofa's armrest, my arms wrapped tightly around my chest, one leg pretzeled around the other, trying unsuccessfully to make myself small enough to disappear as I sputtered out my story. I didn't spare any details, spilling my sins and sorrows and deepest desires to the strangers-turned-friends circled around me.

Three days after my spiral into the dark night of the soul, I was finally able to tell my retreat group about what had transpired that Sabbath morning on the Tuscan hillside. We had gathered in the villa's sunken living room, the cool dimness a welcome refuge from the searing sun and the buzz of mowers and leaf blowers in the garden. Sunk deep into the sofa cushions, my eyes pinned to the floor, I told those gathered about my revelation. Weeping, I choked out the words, a confession of sorts. Fear bubbled to the surface, just as it had three days prior, and along with it, a palpable shame. Surrounded by this cloud of witnesses, I felt embarrassed about my weakness, questions, and doubts. I was deeply ashamed of my lack of faith.

It was quiet in the room when I finally finished talking. Jamin had explained at the start of the retreat that we were to offer each other the space and grace to speak uninterrupted. He had also established some ground rules for responding: ask questions that encourage discernment; offer compassion statements; refrain from giving advice; no hijacking the conversation. Once I finished my story, the community gathered in this quiet circle of trust paused, considering how to respond to my confession in ways that could be both truthful and helpful.

Still sniffling, I finally lifted my eyes from the floor, and when I did, I saw immediately that my story had been received not with judgment, but with compassion. Thirteen faces were turned toward me, and those thirteen men and women, many of whom I had met only a few days before, held me in their embrace. When I saw their faces and looked into their eyes, I glimpsed how God himself looks at me—not with anger, disappointment, or disapproval, but with love.

I don't remember all of the questions and statements that were offered by my fellow group members in response to my

confession that morning, and unfortunately, I was too emo-
tionally unraveled to take notes. I do, however, recall Logan's
response. Sitting across from me on the opposite sofa, she
looked straight into my eyes and declared, "God delights in
you." Logan said more, but what I remember most is that
one proclamation, uttered with unbridled confidence and
authority, like God himself had sidled up next to her on the
sofa and whispered this truth right into her ear. There was
no doubt: Logan believed lock, stock, and barrel that God
delighted in me.

Later, after the trip had ended and we'd all flown back to
our respective home states, Logan reiterated her declaration
in an email. As a quilter, she wrote, she saw the scrappy
quilt, stitched together from leftover pieces of fabric, as a
metaphor for what God was weaving together in me. "Over
and over, when you come to mind," Logan wrote, "I sense
the Lord saying, 'I *really*, *really* like Michelle. I *really*, *really*
love Michelle. And every tiny piece that doesn't seem to go
together is exactly what I have for the beauty of the whole.'"
First in Italy and then later through her email, Logan opened
my eyes to God's presence in me. She gently took my hand
and began to lead me out of the dark night of doubt and into
the light of belief. She helped me see what I'd been blind to;
she helped me believe that God's love is real, not in a general
sense, but specifically and personally, for each and every one
of us, including me.

We can't always see what God is doing in us and through
us. In the midst of our dark night we can't see how he is
using even our most fractured brokenness—the scrappy,
frayed, mismatched, apparently good-for-nothing pieces of
ourselves—for good. But our community helps us see. Our

community guides us when we cannot grope our way through the darkness ourselves. Our community helps us learn to pay better attention to the ways in which God is weaving every part of who we are into a rich, multifaceted, beautiful whole. Our community helps us see how God delights in us, how he *really, really* likes us. How he *really, really* loves us.

Sometimes, when I return home from walking the dog on a winter evening, I pause for a moment in the street before turning down my driveway. I like to pretend I am just someone passing by, a stranger glancing at this white Tudor with the brown trim and the turquoise door. I stand in the cold and watch as the people inside go about their evening rituals—a boy, bent over his homework at the kitchen counter, another upstairs at his computer, a father moving from refrigerator to cabinet, packing lunches for the next day. I notice the watercolor hung above the fireplace, the candle flickering on the mantel, the television tuned to CNN. Lamps are lit in almost every room. Light spills from the windows into the darkness, and as I look in from outside, I see how beautiful it is, this ordinary scene. Yet when I am there in the midst of it, stacking dishes in the dishwasher, hauling a laundry basket up the stairs, wrangling with a child over a math assignment, I so often miss it.

"In true community, we are windows constantly offering each other new views on the mystery of God's presence in our lives," Henri Nouwen wrote.[1] Sometimes we need a window through which to glimpse truth and beauty. Sometimes we need a window through which to glimpse our own belovedness.

Logan was that window to me in Italy. I couldn't see my own belovedness in the moment. Blinded by shame and self-loathing, afraid and alone in my own dark night, I couldn't see that God looked at me with nothing but absolute love and delight. But when Logan matter-of-factly declared God's delight in me, when I could see with my own eyes the truth written all over her face, I began to believe it. In that moment, through that window, I caught a glimpse of "the no matter whatness of God," as Father Greg Boyle calls it.[2] No matter what—no matter our doubts, questions, faults, or sins; no matter our past or present—God loves us. He loved us yesterday, he loves us today, he will love us tomorrow. No matter what.

We can do that for each other. We have the power to be that window for one another, to reflect the "no matter whatness" of God's bottomless, unconditional love for us. With one compassionate word, one tender glance, one empathetic gesture, we can offer each other a brand-new view. We can be the hand that gently leads another from the despair and hopelessness of the dark night into community, intimacy, and light.

## The Journey Outward

First we turn inward, toward God; then we turn outward toward others. We first do the hard and often painful work of pruning toward an open center before we can truly offer anything of ourselves to anyone else. "Communion with God precedes community with others and ministry in the world," said Nouwen. "Once the inward journey has begun, we can move outwardly from solitude to community and ministry."[3]

Discovering and uncovering our true self and our identity as God's most precious Beloved changes everything. Knowing we are loved, no matter what, allows us to release the false sense of self-worth we have clutched for so long. We drop the façade we have clung to so anxiously. Pruned of our unnecessary branches and leaves, our uniquely beautiful, God-created essential self, hidden so long beneath the tangle, now has room to grow free and unencumbered into a new, fuller, more abundant life.

This spaciousness and freedom in Christ in turn allows us, like petals unfurling, to open our tightly clenched fists and our tightly wrapped hearts. Our lives, once propelled by insecurity, self-deceit, and a sense of scarcity and loss, are now God's, and we live into his plan for us with great joy and expectation. As Ann Voskamp says, "When you know you are loved enough, that you are made enough, you have abundantly enough to generously give enough. And that moves you into the enoughness of an even more intimate communion."[4] When we finally cease hustling and striving for our self-worth, when we finally stop trying to build our own kingdoms, we are free and willing to participate as God's servants in building his kingdom on earth. Now our truest desire is to reflect God's love to others, as God's love has been reflected to us.

> This spaciousness and freedom in Christ in turn allows us, like petals unfurling, to open our tightly clenched fists and our tightly wrapped hearts.

This gets at the heart of the question God asked me on the park bench, the question I had slammed shut so many months before. God knew I had spent my whole life using humor, "clowning out," busyness, hustle, and striving to maintain a manageable distance between myself and those closest to me. He knew that lack of intimacy with others was the result of my persistent distrust of him. He knew I would not be able to love others wholly and fully until I first accepted his no-matter-what love for me.

Two weeks before I departed for Tuscany, I read Shannan Martin's book *Falling Free: Rescued from the Life I Always Wanted*. Few books have left more of a lasting impact on me than this one. Shannan writes about her pilgrimage outward from a comfortable, practical life toward a life in authentic community with those living at the margins—the poor, the oppressed, the imprisoned, the downtrodden, the other. Shannan's book convicted me, yet it also left me frustrated. I yearned to "do something" to serve and connect more authentically with marginalized people in my own community, yet I didn't know where or how to begin. I remember leaving Shannan an exasperated Voxer message, describing my desire as well as my frustration. I also remember her response: "Be patient. Keep your eyes and ears open. You will know."

Three months after I returned from Italy, as God was busy pruning, dismantling, revealing, and generally rearranging my life, Brad and I attended a small event here in Lincoln called "True Stories—Live." While I don't recall the specific theme or all the stories the speakers presented from the stage that evening, I do remember Sara's story. Moved by the heartbreaking photograph of Alan Kurdi, the three-year-old Syrian refugee who had washed ashore on a Turkish beach, his red toddler sneakers still on his feet, Sara, an ordinary mother living in ordinary Lincoln, Nebraska, committed to do something. The photograph and the plight of the refugees compelled Sara to become a refugee sponsor and advocate for a local resettlement agency.

I turned to Brad as Sara exited the stage. "I need to do this," I whispered. "I need to do something with this." The next day I friended Sara on Facebook, introduced myself, and found out who to contact at the refugee resettlement agency in town. Within a week, Brad and I had signed up to sponsor a family. Within a month, we had the names of a Yezidi family of six who would be arriving in Lincoln from Iraq. We had three weeks to furnish a home for them.

Preparing the apartment and stockpiling bed linens, dishware, furniture, towels, and kitchen utensils was the easy part. The idea of forging a relationship with a family from a vastly different culture, on the other hand, was significantly more daunting. Our case coordinator told us what she knew about our family, but details were sparse. We learned that the father spoke some English, and that they had at least a few friends and perhaps even family members already living in Lincoln. We were told the family had been forced to flee their home in 2014 during the genocide that had left more than 5,000 Yezidis dead at the hands of ISIS. The family had been living on the run for more than two years.

"You will be their doorway into this new life," our case coordinator told Brad and me, "but your lives are about to be changed forever too." Her comment stopped me short. Truth be told, being "the doorway into a new life" for a family who spoke a different language, practiced a religion that, until three weeks prior, I'd never even heard of, and had suffered inconceivable grief and hardship sounded like a commitment I wasn't sure I wanted to make. As I mentioned earlier, I am triple type A. I like a plan, complete with a spreadsheet, if possible. Instead, I had a single sheet of paper listing six names and birthdates. I couldn't predict what these new relationships would look like. I didn't know how to navigate this new experience. It all felt pretty far beyond the tidy boundaries of my comfortable, ordinary life—a life I wasn't convinced I wanted to change.

## And Who Is My Neighbor?

It's been nearly a year since the frigid December afternoon Azzat, Afia, Yazin, Yara, Dara, and Muntaha stepped through the United Airlines gate and into the terminal of Lincoln Municipal Airport. Our case coordinator had been right. My life has been forever changed.

My family and our Iraqi friends have shared picnics in the park at a table crammed with platters of dolma, kulicha, and naan alongside bags of Doritos, potato salad, and sub sandwiches. We've celebrated birthdays with Super Saver sheet cakes and baklava. We've donned Spiderman and princess costumes and traipsed door-to-door trick-or-treating. We've sat rapt, knee-to-knee on our friends' living room floor, as Azzat described what it was like to flee their home, leaving behind virtually all their possessions, mere hours before ISIS invaded.

Our Yezidi friends have redefined the concept of hospitality for me. The ones who arrived from the other side of the globe with their life's possessions in six suitcases have invited us into their home, their community, and their lives and lavished us with kindness and generosity.

But I wouldn't be honest if I didn't admit that there have also been moments of awkwardness and discomfort. One afternoon, early in our relationship, I stood at the curb with Afia and her kids after driving them home from a doctor's appointment. Afia doesn't speak English and I don't speak Kurdish, so our communication typically involves a lot of gesticulating, miming, and smiling. When she blew me a kiss, I assumed that was how Yezidis said goodbye. So I blew a kiss back, only to realize mid-kiss that Afia had in fact been trying to communicate an invitation to come inside for a bite to eat and was *not* blowing kisses at me. I shook my head, feeling my face redden and laughing awkwardly as I struggled to decline the invitation as graciously as possible. I felt more than a little stupid and embarrassed as I drove away.

What I'm learning, slowly but surely, is that God doesn't call us to be comfortable. Page through the Bible from Genesis to Revelation, and you won't find many stories of easy-breezy smooth sailing. What you will find is story after story of people who step out of their comfort zones, people who move toward others in community, people who take risks and take a stand, people who bend low to lift someone else up, even when—and sometimes especially when—that person is different from them.

No biblical story illustrates this better than the parable of the Good Samaritan, which was prompted by a conversation between Jesus and a religious scholar (see Luke 10:25–37). "Teacher," the scholar asked Jesus one day, "what should I do to inherit eternal life?" (v. 25 NLT). Jesus responded to the question as he often did, with a question of his own: "What does the law of Moses say? How do you read it?" (v. 26 NLT). Jesus' question was a no-brainer, the entry-level round in a Scripture quiz show, and the scholar was quick with his response. "'You must love the LORD your God with all your heart, all your soul, all your strength, and all your mind.' And, 'Love your neighbor as yourself'" (v. 27 NLT), he answered, reciting Deuteronomy 6:5, a verse that had been emblazoned in his memory since childhood.

We would expect the conversation to end at that point. The scholar had answered the question correctly, and Jesus praised him, assuring the man that if he followed the command to love God and love his neighbor as himself, he would live. Unsatisfied, the scholar, however, pressed Jesus with a follow-up question: "And who is my neighbor?" (v. 29 NLT).

As numerous biblical commentators have noted, the man wanted Jesus to identify not who *was* his neighbor, but who *wasn't* his neighbor. In other words, the religious expert was asking, "Which people can I exclude? Which people don't count? Which people fall outside the realm of neighbor?" "In ancient culture, as today, such boundaries might have run along ethnic lines," explains one commentator. "There was a category of 'non-neighbor,' and the lawyer is seeking Jesus' endorsement of that concept. In contemporary terms, any of various forms of racism may underlie the scribe's question: there are neighbors, 'my folk,' and then there are the rest, 'them.'"[5]

The fact that a Samaritan took center stage in Jesus' story undoubtedly shocked the Jews who were listening to this exchange. Considered "half-breeds," the Samaritans, who were half-Jewish, half-Gentile, were despised by the Jews, and the two groups had a long history of tension and conflict. No Jew would have considered a Samaritan his neighbor, which is exactly why Jesus made the Samaritan the hero of his story. Jesus did an about-face with his listeners' expectations; in his story, the "bad guy" was the hero.

In the parable, a Jewish man traveling the seventeen-mile journey from Jerusalem to Jericho along a notoriously dangerous thoroughfare is robbed, beaten, and left for dead alongside the road. The first person to pass by is a priest, but surprisingly, the priest does not stop to help the injured man. Instead, he crosses to the other side of the street, going as far out of his way as possible so as not to be bothered or delayed. The second person to appear is a Levite, someone who served in the temple. But like the priest before him, the Levite notices the injured man and then, crossing to the far side of the street, passes him by without a second glance.

Finally, Jesus told those gathered around him, "a despised Samaritan" (Luke 10:33 NLT) comes along. Seeing the injured man's appalling condition, the Samaritan's "heart went out to him" (Luke 10:33 Message). The Samaritan approaches the injured Jewish man, his supposed enemy, tends to his wounds, transports the man on his own donkey to a nearby inn, and then pays a substantial amount of money for the man's lodging. In fact, as one commentator notes, the two denarii—equivalent to two days' wages—that the Samaritan leaves with the innkeeper is enough to cover a three-week stay.[6] In other words, the Samaritan doesn't do the bare minimum; he goes above and beyond his neighborly duty.

The moral of the story is obvious, even to the religious scholar, who, though he couldn't bring himself to utter the word "Samaritan" out loud, admitted to Jesus that the neighbor in this story was "the one who showed [the injured man] mercy." "Yes," Jesus answered the religious expert, "now go and do the same" (Luke 10:37 NLT).

Truth be told, on most days, I'm right there with the religious scholar. I limit my neighborhood to the places in which I am most comfortable. I limit my definition of neighbor to the people who look like me, think like me, talk like me, vote like me, worship like me, and have the same interests I have. It's easier that way—neater, less awkward, less fraught, less frightening. There's less chance of making mistakes with the people and places I already know, less opportunity for failure, conflict, or embarrassment. But when I stay safe-at-an-arm's-length away from people I don't know and places I don't ordinarily go, there's also infinitely less potential for encountering the richness and beauty of God's vast kingdom in all its infinite variety. Jesus calls us to step into the unfamiliar, the uncomfortable, the awkward, and the just plain messy to be a neighbor. Jesus knows that just beyond our discomfort, we will discover unexpected beauty, grace, and, above all, community.

> Jesus calls us to step into the unfamiliar, the uncomfortable, the awkward, and the just plain messy to be a neighbor. Jesus knows that just beyond our discomfort, we will discover unexpected beauty, grace, and, above all, community.

## When "Us" and "Them" Become One

Stepping toward someone outside your comfortable place doesn't necessarily have to be as complicated as the Good Samaritan story. I think sometimes we assume that loving our neighbor should involve big, dramatic gestures or actions. But focusing only on the big and the dramatic results in lost opportunities for a simpler but no less real connection.

"Give a cool cup of water to someone who is thirsty, for instance. The smallest act of giving or receiving makes you a true apprentice. You won't lose a thing," Jesus reminds us (Matt. 10:42 Message). We offer a cup of water to someone who is thirsty—thirsty for actual water, thirsty for companionship, thirsty for a listening ear. We reach out to carry another's burden or simply stand alongside someone suffering through a season of grief, hardship, or heartache. We share a pot of soup or a platter of dolma. We pass the bag of chips. We play Frisbee, kick a soccer ball back and forth, laugh until our ribs ache. We don't lose a thing; our giving is our gain.

One late-summer afternoon we met our Yezidi friends for a picnic at the park. Numerous rounds of Frisbee, a feast of epic proportions, one bee sting, and hours of swinging, sliding, and seesawing later, the two older girls and I were sitting spent and sweaty on a bench when suddenly, nine-year-old Dara reached up to touch my hair. The three girls constantly marvel over how short I wear it. Yezidi women and girls typically have very long hair, so I'm pretty certain Dara, Yara, and Mun have never seen a woman with hair as cropped as mine. As she stroked my head, Dara exclaimed in delight, "You have guinea pig hair!" We all laughed hard at that one, and later her dad, Azzat, apologized, explaining that his kids don't always know what's culturally appropriate yet. I assured him that I couldn't have been more delighted. After all, earlier that afternoon Dara had confided that guinea pigs are hands-down her favorite animals. I knew that to be told I have the hair of a guinea pig was to receive the highest compliment.

I admit straight up, I had a savior complex when I first signed on to sponsor a refugee family. I imagined myself something of a hero, swooping in to make everything better. I half-expected our family to step off the plane with dust caking their clothes and rubble in their hair. There was "us"—my husband and me and our friends who gathered furniture and household items to set up the apartment—and "them," the poor refugees who would benefit from and be grateful for our generosity.

The desire to be the Good Samaritan, to help someone less fortunate than ourselves, is good. But as Father Greg Boyle writes, "Often we strike the high moral distance that separates 'us' from 'them.' Yet it is God's dream come true when we recognize that there exists no daylight between us. Serving others is good. It's a start. But it's just the hallway that leads to the Grand Ballroom."[7]

My desire to help a refugee family and our efforts to furnish an apartment for them was a good start; it was a step into the hallway. But sitting cross-legged on the carpet knee-to-knee with new friends, passing platters of dolma and naan? Singing Happy Birthday together and coloring princess pictures? Laughing with a nine-year-old Yezidi girl over guinea pig hair? That is the Grand Ballroom—the place we step into when we walk toward community, the place where the divisions between "us" and "them" fall away and we simply come together as one. The Grand Ballroom is the place not only where someone else's life is changed, but the place where our lives are changed forever too.

It seems counterintuitive, but trees that grow closely together in a forest—even those of different species—are more likely to survive and thrive than those with ample space between them. Rather than competing for natural resources, as one would expect, trees that are tucked closely together nurture and support each other, synchronizing their rates of photosynthesis and parceling out water and nutrients via their root systems so that all can be equally successful.

This surprised Peter Wohlleben, who, as a commercial forester, had been trained to thin out trees in his forests in order to give the strongest, healthiest trees the best chance to flourish by providing them with more space and more access to sunlight. He later learned, however, that forests are more resilient when the trees are packed tightly together.

We look at a forest with our untrained eyes, and we see what we assume are individual entities—pines, firs, oaks, beeches, chestnuts, lindens—different species of trees in direct competition with one another. What we don't see is that beneath the soil, something much more complex is taking place.

Back in the mid-nineties, scientists discovered the mycorrhizal network, a labyrinth of fungi entwined among tree roots. Nicknamed the "wood wide web," this network is composed of microscopic threads called *hyphae*. Woven into the tips of plant roots at a cellular level, hyphae operate like fiber-optic internet cables, connecting trees with their neighbors. One teaspoon of forest soil can contain miles of hyphae, and over centuries, a single fungus can network an entire forest over hundreds of acres, according to Wohlleben and other scientists.[8]

Both the trees and the fungi benefit from their symbiotic relationship. The fungi syphon some of the carbon-rich sugar that the trees produce during photosynthesis, and the trees obtain phosphorus and nitrogen that the fungi acquire from the soil. But, scientists have discovered, the relationship between trees and fungi goes far beyond symbiosis. The mycorrhizal network also allows trees to distribute nutrients between one another. So, for example, a dying tree may sacrifice its resources for the benefit of the community, or a young seedling struggling for sunlight in the understory might be supported with extra resources by its taller neighbors.[9] In addition, trees use the wood wide web to exchange news about insect infestation, drought, and other dangers. In the end, as Peter Wohlleben says, "A tree can be only as strong as the forest that surrounds it."[10]

Turns out, we humans are more like trees than you might expect. "All of you together are Christ's body," Paul reminded the Corinthians, "and each of you is a part of it" (1 Cor. 12:27 NLT). Like trees, our well-being depends in large part on our connection with and integration into our community. We need each other for nourishment, connection, and support. We sustain each other through seasons of drought; we hold each other up as violent storms rage around us; we flourish together in seasons of abundance. Like a tree that is only as strong as the forest that surrounds it, we humans thrive best together. Or, as Paul put it, "No matter how significant you are, it is only because of what you are a *part* of" (1 Cor. 12:19 Message).

The Japanese maple I wrote about at the beginning of this book is a magnificent tree, to be sure, but it's made all the more spectacular by its place in the garden as a whole. The mossy paths and the hand-raked gravel, the stately sculpture and rotund boulders, the perfectly coiffed azalea, the whispering waterfalls and reflective ponds, the delicately arched bridge, and the teahouse tucked into the quiet glade—all are individual elements intended to function as part of a harmonic whole, each piece melding with the others to create an overall atmosphere of tranquility and unity in the garden. Even the view of downtown Portland's skyscrapers in the distance is woven into the overall design of the landscape. The beauty and originality of each element is impacted and magnified by its relation to the other features around it. Water, wood, air, and stone all exist in harmony, with no single element more important than another or the whole.

The process of pruning to an open center is, in the end, not an isolated, solitary endeavor. While much of our inner work happens alone with God in solitude and stillness, pruning open—the journey toward uncovering and discovering our true self—takes place within a much larger context. The purpose of pruning open is ultimately not only about uncovering our true self, but also about coming to recognize and understand our place in God's kingdom on earth. When we know who we are, when we know we are loved unabashedly by God, no matter what, we can't help but recognize that love in others, and we yearn to reflect God's love back to them.

Like the water, wood, air, and stone of a Japanese garden, like the trees growing next to one another in the forest—

branches touching, roots entwined—we are better together. We belong to each other. We are part of each other. We are better together because God created us for community.

Recently I watched my sixteen-year-old son link hands with Afia and take his place in a long line of dancers. I watched him smile self-consciously, stumbling a bit, eyes on his feet as he attempted to master the steps of a traditional Yezidi dance along with hundreds of Iraqi men and women. All around us the air was filled with language we couldn't understand and music we didn't recognize. My husband, our two sons, and I were in the minority, four of less than a dozen non-Yezidis present at the New Year's festivities that day, an experience that was at the same time a little bit awkward and wholly beautiful.

What does it look like to recognize God's love in the face of someone who doesn't look like you, in the voice of someone whose language you cannot speak or understand? What does it look like to live in community side by side with someone different from you? What does it look like to know you are loved by God, to share that love with another, and, in turn, to receive God's love from that person? Truthfully, it looks a lot like my sixteen-year-old son stumbling through the steps of an unfamiliar dance. It looks like stepping on each other's toes from time to time. It looks like nervous laughter, self-conscious smiles, sweaty palms. It looks like two steps forward, one step back. This is the Grand Ballroom, as Father Boyle says—the place we grab the hand of another and step from the narrow hallway of "us" and "them" into the wide-open, spacious "withness" of kinship and community. When we dance in the Grand Ballroom, we enter into the mystery of God's presence, reflected back to us in the person we least expect to find it.

shaping

## GOING DEEPER

The journey toward true self does not end in an inward place. Ultimately God beckons us outward into community, where we participate in God's perfect plan for his kingdom on earth. God invites us into intimate relationship with him, to know him and to know ourselves in him, so that we may then live more compassionately and intimately with those around us. We are the windows, as Henri Nouwen said, through which others may glimpse God. They are windows through which we might glimpse God.

Consider these questions as you step from the small room inside yourself, down the hallway of serving, and finally, into the Grand Ballroom of community and kinship:

1. Ponder Paul's words to the Corinthians: "No matter how significant you are, it is only because of what you are a *part* of" (1 Cor. 12:19 Message). Consider the communities you are part of. How have they shaped you, influenced you, and impacted you?

2. Read the parable of the Good Samaritan (Luke 10:25–37) slowly and reflectively, aloud if possible. Try to place yourself in the story as you read it. Is there one particular character—the priest, the Levite, the injured man, the Samaritan, a bystander, the religious scholar who is questioning Jesus—with whom you relate? Is there a

particular person or group of people in your own life whom you disqualify as a neighbor?

3. Consider Henri Nouwen's observation that "we are windows constantly offering each other new views on the mystery of God's presence in our lives." Who has been that window to you in your life? Is there someone for whom you could be a window to God's presence? What would that look like, practically speaking?

4. If you are currently ministering to or serving a particular group or person, what's one step you could take to begin to walk down the hallway into the Grand Ballroom of true community and kinship?

# epilogue

Leaning against the winter sky, she began her vigil
of trust.

—Macrina Wiederkehr, *Seasons of Your Heart*

It's late November again, and I'm back at the bench. I haven't
sat here as often these last few weeks. Lately, when Josie tugs
toward our spot, I pull her along. "No bench today," I tell
her. "We've got too much to do." I've fallen back into my
old bad habits—rushing on to the next thing, mind reeling,
heart racing.

Still, when I finally decide to stop and sit today, my breathing slows, my posture softens, and my mind relaxes easily
into rest. Turns out, I haven't forgotten. My body and soul
remember this quiet place on the far side of the wilderness.

It's warm for November. The remnants of the wildflowers
sway in the ravine, and a few leaves summersault across the
path, but otherwise it is still. I notice the tree that lost a limb

in a summer storm a few months ago has been cut back with a chainsaw, sawdust scattered at the stump. I wonder where the red-bellied woodpecker will find its food now; this tree with its rotted trunk was a favorite.

It feels good to rest. I think about the journey that began on this bench, with five minutes of silence and an uncomfortable question that rose unbidden from the depths. The pruning open continues. I haven't dropped all my camouflaging leaves, cut all my brambly branches. I still wrestle with my faith and with who I am. I still wonder, sometimes, if I have uncovered my true self.

The truth is, we'll always be uncovering, pruning, shaping, and opening toward our center. We'll release our leaves, prune away our branches, clip back the persistent suckers, nurture our tender shoots, entwine our roots and branches with those of our neighbors. We'll cycle through this process with the seasons. Sometimes we will wonder if we've changed at all.

And yet, bit by bit, perhaps without even noticing, we will come closer to our center, closer to God. "Pruning is an exercise of relationship," observes gardener Tricia Smyth. "We ask the tree within its nature to adapt to our needs. We in turn provide all that is needed for the tree to thrive."[1] The same can be said for spiritual pruning to an open center; it, too, is an exercise of relationship between us and God. God asks that we live into the beautiful, beloved persons he created us to be; he gives us what we need to bloom into our truest, most authentic selves and then to join ourselves with our community.

Today as I pause at the bench, I notice the trees. They are bare, their branches skeletal against a slate November sky.

All except the oaks, that is. Fully clad, brown leaves curled crisp, the oaks, I know, will hold on to their covering as long as possible—for at least another month or more.

As I sit, a breeze lifts the branches high above my head. The oak leaves dance, twirling on their stems. I tip my head back, watching from the bench as a single tiny brown leaf lets go. It spins to the ground, settling in the grass near my feet.

The smallest of beginnings has begun again.

# appendix

**Practical Tips for Establishing a Practice of Directed Rest**

1. **Start small.** Five or ten minutes of quiet stillness is plenty. You are much more likely to stick with a daily practice if you begin with a manageable amount of time. You can always increase the time you spend in directed rest as you grow more comfortable with the practice.

2. **Pick a comfortable, accessible spot away from distractions.** This location may be a short distance from your home, like my park bench, or it could be a corner of your own backyard or living room. The key is to identify a place that is away, physically and/or mentally, from distraction, but also accessible enough that you'll be less likely to make excuses for skipping the practice.

3. **Integrate your directed rest into an already-existing daily routine.** Identify a slice of time in your schedule that you could dedicate to directed rest, rather than

trying to manufacture a whole new ritual. For example, I slipped my five minutes of directed rest into my daily routine of walking the dog. I was already walking the dog anyway, so it didn't take much effort to weave five minutes of directed rest into that time. You may find five minutes while you wait to pick up your kids from school, during your daily lunch break at the office, or during an after-dinner walk.

4. **Keep it simple.** The more complicated you make this practice, the more difficult it will be to keep it up. Lighting a special candle or diffusing a particular scent can be lovely touches, but in the end, if you have to jump through too many hoops just to prepare to sit for five minutes, you may not end up sitting at all.

5. **Aim for twenty-one consecutive days.** Research indicates that it takes a minimum of three weeks to form a new habit. Aim for twenty-one consecutive days of directed rest right out of the gate before you allow yourself to skip a day, and you'll be more likely to keep up the practice in the long term.

6. **Set a timer or an alarm,** especially if, like me, you are inclined to pick up your phone to look at the time every two minutes. Knowing your alarm will go off when the five minutes are up will help you resist the urge to look.

7. **Be silent.** This probably goes without saying, but silence means no music or podcasts in your earbuds, no texting, scrolling social media, or talking on the phone. If you can, keep your phone out of sight, and turn off notifications so you won't be tempted to check Facebook or respond to the ding of an incoming text "just this one time."

8. **Focus your attention on your immediate surroundings.** Be present in the moment. What do you smell? What sounds do you hear? What do you see? Grounding yourself in the now will help to keep your mind from pinballing from one distracted thought to the next. You'll also be amazed by how much you've missed as you've scurried to accomplish every item on your never-ending to-do list.

9. **Be kind to yourself.** Your mind *will* flit from thought to thought, especially in the early days and weeks of beginning this practice. But remember, there is really no right or wrong way to do this, so try not to berate yourself if it feels hard or if it looks like you are failing. If your brain leaps ahead to the future or backtracks to the past, simply bring it back to the present by noticing and acknowledging what's right in front of you.

10. **Lower your expectations.** You may not experience a life-changing revelation right away. In fact, you may not *ever* experience a life-changing revelation. Remember, the point of this is not to do or produce, but to be—to allow the time and space for whatever might be churning below the surface to rise up. It may take some time, but you will hear your soul speak if you offer it the opportunity to do so. What your soul says, on the other hand, may not be what you expect.

11. **Finally, enjoy it!** These five or ten minutes of solitude and silence are for you—a time to begin to know your true self, a time in which you will begin to uncover the person God created you to be. Allow yourself the opportunity to enjoy these few minutes as God's gift to you, his Beloved.

# notes

1. Macrina Wiederkehr, *Seasons of Your Heart: Prayers and Reflections, Revised and Expanded* (New York: HarperCollins, 1991), 8.

## Part I Know the Tree

1. Judy Maier, "Revealing the 'Essence of the Tree': Aesthetic Pruning of Japanese Maples," *Pacific Horticulture* 73, no. 1 (Jan. 2012), http://www.pacific horticulture.org/articles/revealing-the-essence-of-the-tree-aesthetic-pruning -of-japanese-maples/.

## Chapter 1 Leaves and Branches

1. Gene Weingarten, "Pearls before Breakfast: Can One of the Nation's Great Musicians Cut through the Fog of a DC Rush Hour? Let's Find Out," *Washington Post Magazine*, April 8, 2007, https://www.washingtonpost.com/lifestyle/maga zine/pearls-before-breakfast-can-one-of-the-nations-great-musicians-cut-through -the-fog-of-a-dc-rush-hour-lets-find-out/2014/09/23/8a6d46da-4331-11e4-b47c -f5889e061e5f_story.html?utm_term=.ff81c02b64b0.

2. Ibid.

3. Ibid.

4. Ibid.

5. The Enneagram Institute, https://www.enneagraminstitute.com/type-3/.

6. "The State of American Vacation 2017," Project: Time Off, May 23, 2017, https://projecttimeoff.com/reports/the-state-of-american-vacation-2017/.

7. Gillian Coutts, "Feeling Stressed and Unproductive? Here's How to Stop Being Busy and Be Mindful Instead," Smart Company, February 12, 2016, http://www .smartcompany.com.au/finance/62947-feeling-stressed-and-unproductive-heres -how-to-stop-being-busy-and-be-mindful-instead/.

8. John Ortberg, *Soul Keeping: Caring for the Most Important Part of You* (Grand Rapids: Zondervan, 2014), 59.

9. Ibid.

10. Dr. Caroline Leaf, *Switch On Your Brain: The Key to Peak Happiness, Thinking, and Health* (Grand Rapids: Baker Books, 2013), 83.

11. Ibid., 84.

## Chapter 2  Beneath the Canopy

1. "David Tutor Performs John Cage's 4'33", 1952, Artforum video, https://www.artforum.com/video/id=21612&mode=large&page_id=18.

2. Richard Kostelantz, *Conversations with Cage* (New York: Limelight Editions, 1988), 65–66.

3. Leaf, *Switch On Your Brain*, 82.

4. Maier, "Revealing the 'Essence of the Tree.'"

5. Ruth Haley Barton, *Invitation to Solitude and Silence: Experiencing God's Transforming Presence* (Downers Grove, IL: InterVarsity, 2004), 96.

6. Parker Palmer, *Let Your Life Speak: Listening for the Voice of Vocation* (San Francisco: Jossey-Bass, 2000), 7–8.

7. Adam McHugh, *The Listening Life: Embracing Attentiveness in a World of Distraction* (Downers Grove, IL: InterVarsity, 2015), 181.

## Chapter 3  Broken Limbs

1. Richard Rohr, *Falling Upward: A Spirituality for the Two Halves of Life* (San Francisco: Jossey-Bass, 2011), ix.

2. Ibid., xvii.

3. Mark Buchanan, *The Rest of God: Restoring Your Soul by Restoring Sabbath* (Nashville: Thomas Nelson, 2006), 190.

4. Dallas Willard, *Hearing God: Developing a Conversational Relationship with God* (Downers Grove, IL: InterVarsity, 2012), 130–31.

5. Rohr, *Falling Upward*, 21.

6. Ruth Haley Barton, *Sacred Rhythms: Arranging Our Lives for Spiritual Transformation* (Downers Grove, IL: InterVarsity, 2006), 27.

7. Ibid., 22.

8. Ibid.

9. Barton, *Invitation to Solitude and Silence*, 50–51.

## Chapter 4  Seeds of Desire

1. Enneagram Institute, https://www.enneagraminstitute.com/type-3.

2. Thomas Merton, *Seeds of Contemplation* (New York: New Directions, 1986), 28.

3. Barton, *Invitation to Solitude and Silence*, 50.

4. Ibid., 96.

## Part II  *Fukinaoshi* of the Soul

1. Jake Hobson, *Niwaki: Pruning, Training and Shaping Trees the Japanese Way* (Portland, OR: Timber Press, 2007), 49.

## Chapter 5  The Hard Prune

1. Brian Kolodiejchuk, *Mother Teresa: Come Be My Light: The Private Writings of the Saint of Calcutta* (New York: Doubleday, 2007), 163.

2. Ibid., 210.

3. St. John of the Cross, *Dark Night of the Soul*, trans. by E. Allison Peers, from the critical edition of P. Silverio de Santa Teresa, C.D. (New York: Dover Publications, 2003), 8, 78.

4. Barton, *Invitation to Solitude and Silence*, 104.

5. Hobson, *Niwaki*, 50.

6. Kolodiejchuk, *Mother Teresa*, 192–93.

7. Richard Rohr, "Mystery Is Endless Knowability," Center for Action and Contemplation, August 23, 2016, https://cac.org/mystery-endless-knowability-2016-08-23/.

8. Larry Crabb, "God Meets Us Where We Are . . . ," Larry Crabb's New-Way Ministries Blog, November 2, 2011, https://newwaymin.wordpress.com/2011/11/02/god-meets-us-where-we-are/.

9. Ortberg, *Soul Keeping*, 65.

10. Rohr, "Mystery Is Endless Knowability."

11. Eugene Peterson, *A Long Obedience in the Same Direction: Discipleship in an Instant Society* (Downers Grove, IL: InterVarsity, 2000), 30.

12. Henri Nouwen, *The Way of the Heart* (San Francisco: HarperSanFrancisco, 1981), 27.

13. Blue Letter Bible, accessed May 21, 2018, https://www.blueletterbible.org/lang/lexicon/lexicon.cfm?t=kjv&strongs=h3290.

14. Blue Letter Bible, accessed May 21, 2018, https://www.blueletterbible.org/lang/lexicon/lexicon.cfm?strongs=H6117&t=KJV.

15. Bible Study Tools, accessed May 21, 2018, https://www.biblestudytools.com/lexicons/hebrew/kjv/aqob.html.

16. Barton, *Invitation to Solitude and Silence*, 93.

17. Mark Buchanan, *Spiritual Rhythm: Being with Jesus Every Season of Your Soul* (Grand Rapids: Zondervan, 2010), 50.

18. Rainer Maria Rilke, *Letters to a Young Poet* (Novato, CA: New World Library, 2000), 35.

## Chapter 6  The Far Side of the Wilderness

1. Thomas Merton, *Thoughts in Solitude* (New York: Farrar, Straus & Giroux, 1956), 96.

2. Ibid., 79.

3. Barbara Brown Taylor, *Learning to Walk in the Dark* (New York: HarperCollins, 2014), 87.

4. Sue Monk Kidd, *When the Heart Waits: Spiritual Direction for Life's Sacred Questions* (San Francisco: HarperSanFrancisco, 1992), 136.

## Chapter 7  Rooted

1. Elizabeth J. Canham, "A School for the Lord's Service," *Weavings* 9 (January–February 1995), 15; as quoted in Jane Tomaine, *St. Benedict's Toolbox: The Nuts*

*and Bolts of Everyday Benedictine Living* (Harrisburg, PA: Morehouse Publishing, 2005), 45.

2. Daniel K. Eisenbud, "Ancient Tablets Reveal Daily Life of Exiled Jews in Babylon 2,500 Years Ago," *Jerusalem Post*, February 5, 2015, http://www.jpost.com/Not-Just-News/Ancient-tablets-reveal-daily-life-of-exiled-Jews-in-Babylon-2500-years-ago-389864.

3. Ibid.

4. Tomaine, *St. Benedict's Toolbox*, 46.

5. Hobson, *Niwaki*, 49.

6. Canham, "A School for the Lord's Service," 15; as quoted in Tomaine, *St. Benedict's Toolbox*, 83.

7. Kidd, *When the Heart Waits*, 132.

8. Richard Rohr, *The Naked Now: Learning to See as the Mystics See* (New York: Crossroad Publishing Company, 2009), 142.

9. Ann Voskamp, *The Broken Way: A Daring Path into the Abundant Life* (Grand Rapids: Zondervan, 2016), 75.

10. Brennan Manning, *Abba's Child: The Cry of the Heart for Intimate Belonging* (Colorado Springs: NavPress, 2015), 34–35.

## Part III  Shaping

1. Hobson, *Niwaki*, 52.

## Chapter 8  Twine and Splint

1. Timothy Keller, *Counterfeit Gods: The Empty Promise of Money, Sex, and Power, and the Only Hope That Matters* (New York: Penguin, 2009), xviii.

2. Emily Dickinson, "I'm Nobody, Who Are You?" in *Poems by Emily Dickinson: Second Series*, eds. T. W. Higginson and Mabel Loomis Todd (Boston: Roberts Brothers, 1891), 21.

3. Henry David Thoreau, *Life without Principle*, 1863, http://xroads.virginia.edu/~hyper2/thoreau/life.html.

4. Richard Rohr, *Immortal Diamond: The Search for Our True Self* (San Francisco: Jossey-Bass, 2013), 52.

5. Lee Reich, "How To: Removing Root Suckers," Fine Gardening, http://www.finegardening.com/video-removing-root-suckers.

6. Hobson, *Niwaki*, 52.

7. Richard Foster, *Celebration of Discipline: The Path to Spiritual Growth* (New York: HarperCollins, 1998), 7.

8. Shinrin-yoku.org, http://www.shinrin-yoku.org/shinrin-yoku.html.

9. Carolyn Gregoire, "The New Science of the Creative Brain on Nature," *Outside*, March 18, 2016, https://www.outsideonline.com/2062221/new-science-creative-brain-nature.

10. Ibid.

11. Quoted in Charles J. Healy, *Praying with the Jesuits: Finding God in All Things* (Mahwah, NJ: Paulist, 2011), 45.

## Chapter 9  Way Opens

1. Palmer, *Let Your Life Speak*, 12.
2. Philip Gulley, "Quaker Sayings 5: Proceed as the Way Opens," accessed October 23, 2017, http://philipgulley.com/wp-content/uploads/2013/07/Quaker-Sayings-5.pdf.
3. Author Dani Shapiro offered this quote from Dolly Parton in her interview on The Beautiful Writers podcast, episode entitled "Jennifer Rudolph Walsh on Together-ness," accessed October 23, 2017, https://soundcloud.com/user-780938996/jennifer-walsh-on-together-ness.
4. Literary agent Jennifer Rudolph Walsh offered this quote from Mark Twain in her interview on The Beautiful Writers podcast, episode entitled "Jennifer Rudolph Walsh on Together-ness," accessed October 23, 2017, https://soundcloud.com/user-780938996/jennifer-walsh-on-together-ness.
5. Palmer, *Let Your Life Speak*, 13.
6. Merton, *Thoughts in Solitude*, 69.
7. "Michelangelo's Prisoners or Slaves," Accademia.org, http://www.accademia.org/explore-museum/artworks/michelangelos-prisoners-slaves/.
8. James M. Saslow, *The Poetry of Michelangelo: An Annotated Translation* (New Haven: Yale University Press, 1991), 35.
9. As quoted in Barbara Brown Taylor, *Learning to Walk in the Dark* (New York: HarperCollins, 2014), 179.
10. Brené Brown, *The Gifts of Imperfection: Let Go of Who You Think You're Supposed to Be and Embrace Who You Are* (Center City, MN: Hazelden, 2010), xiv.
11. Eric Liddell quote from *Chariots of Fire*, http://www.imdb.com/title/tt0082158/quotes.
12. Frederick Buechner, *Wishful Thinking: A Seeker's ABC* (New York: HarperCollins, 1993), 119.
13. Cultivated Podcast, "Andy Crouch, Part 2" (episode 12), February 7, 2017, http://www.harbormedia.com/blog/2017/2/6/episode-12-andy-crouch-part-2.
14. "The Inner Landscape of Beauty," *On Being*, August 6, 2015; https://onbeing.org/programs/john-odonohue-the-inner-landscape-of-beauty/.
15. Mary Oliver, "The Summer Day," https://www.loc.gov/poetry/180/133.html.

## Chapter 10  Water, Wood, Air, and Stone

1. Henri Nouwen, *Making All Things New: An Invitation to the Spiritual Life* (San Francisco: HarperOne, 2009), 87.
2. Gregory Boyle, *Tattoos on the Heart: The Power of Boundless Compassion* (New York: Free Press, 2011), 60.
3. Henri Nouwen, *Spiritual Formation: Following the Movements of the Spirit* (New York: HarperCollins, 2010), 124.
4. Voskamp, *The Broken Way*, 68–69.
5. "Discipleship: Looking to Our Neighbor, to Jesus, and to God," Luke 10: IVP New Testament Commentaries, Bible Gateway, https://www.biblegateway.com/resources/commentaries/IVP-NT/Luke/Discipleship-Looking-Our-Jesus.

6. Ibid.

7. Boyle, *Tattoos on the Heart*, 188.

8. Peter Wohlleben, *The Hidden Life of Trees* (Vancouver, BC, Canada: Greystone Books, 2016), 10.

9. Robert Macfarlane, "The Secrets of the Wood Wide Web," *New Yorker*, August 7, 2016, https://www.newyorker.com/tech/elements/the-secrets-of-the-wood-wide-web.

10. Wohlleben, *Hidden Life of Trees*, 17.

### Epilogue

1. Tricia Smyth, "Aesthetic Pruning of Japanese Maples," Essence of the Tree, https://www.essenceofthetree.com/articles/aesthetic-pruning-of-japanese-maples/.

**Michelle DeRusha** is the author of *Katharina and Martin Luther*, *50 Women Every Christian Should Know*, and the memoir *Spiritual Misfit*. She publishes a monthly column about everyday faith for the *Lincoln Journal Star* and offers guidance on listening to your soul on her website, www .michellederusha.com. She lives with her husband and their two boys in Lincoln, Nebraska.

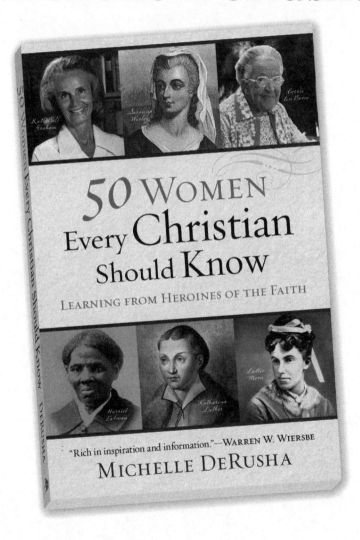
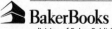

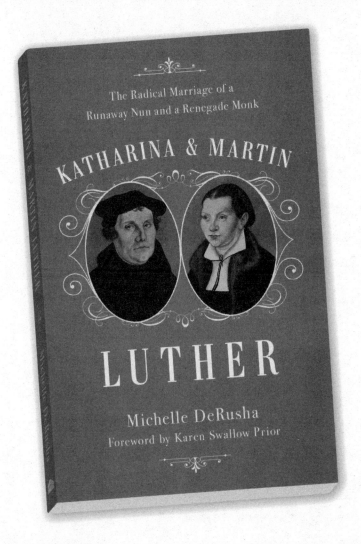

# Meet Michelle!

# MichelleDeRusha.com

Visit Michelle online to receive free downloadables, keep up with her blog, follow along on social media, and much more.

f @MichelleDeRushaAuthor  🐦 @MichelleDeRusha

𝒫 @MichelleDeRusha  📷 @MichelleDeRusha

# LIKE THIS
# BOOK?
## Consider sharing it with others!

---

- Share or mention the book on your social media platforms. Use the hashtag **#TrueYou**.

- Write a book review on your blog or on a retailer site.

- Pick up a copy for friends, family, or anyone who you think would enjoy and be challenged by its message!

- Share this message on Facebook: **I loved #TrueYou by @MichelleDeRushaAuthor // @ReadBakerBooks**

- Share this message on Twitter or Instagram: **I loved #TrueYou by @MichelleDeRusha // @ReadBakerBooks**

- Recommend this book for your church, workplace, book club, or class.

- Follow Baker Books on social media and tell us what you like.

 Facebook.com/ReadBakerBooks

 @ReadBakerBooks